Dear reader,

Thank you for your interest in this booklet of recipes created by our readers, and submitted for our 2013 contest. The winning entries were published in the March 2013 issue of our magazines, and are featured on the first three pages of this booket.

Many other excellent recipes were submitted. They are printed in no particular order and, unlike the winners, were not "kitchen tested" by Ruralite staff.

Thank you again for your interest.

The Winners

White Chocolate Bread Pudding

1 loaf deli French bread
1 qt. half-and-half
3 eggs
2 c. sugar
1 tsp. vanilla
1 stick butter

Cut bread into ½-inch squares in large bowl. Mix eggs, sugar, vanilla and half-and-half. Pour over bread. Let set until moist. Pour mixture into a greased 9-by-12-inch casserole dish. Top with butter cut into squares.

Set dish on a cookie sheet and bake at 350 degrees for 50 minutes.

Sauce:

1 box Baker's white chocolate
1 stick butter
1 cup powdered sugar
1 teaspoon vanilla
Up to 6 teaspoons water
Pecans, chopped

Melt chocolate and butter in microwave. Be careful not to burn. Add remaining ingredients and mix. Pour over baked pudding. Top with chopped pecans.

Frances Hodge
Milton, Florida • Escambia River Electric Cooperative

Baked French Toast

1 day-old loaf French bread
3 eggs
3 Tbsp. sugar
1 tsp. vanilla extract
2¼ c. milk
½ c. flour
6 Tbsp. brown sugar
½ tsp. ground cinnamon
¼ c. butter
1 c. fresh or frozen blueberries
1 c. sliced strawberries

Grease a 9-by-13-inch baking dish. Diagonally cut bread into 1-inch slices and place in a baking dish.

In a medium bowl, lightly beat eggs, sugar and vanilla. Stir in milk until well blended. Pour mixture over bread in baking dish, turning slices to coat well. Cover and refrigerate overnight.

Heat oven to 375 degrees. In a small bowl, combine flour, brown sugar and cinnamon. Cut in butter until mixture resembles coarse crumbs.

Turn bread slices over in the baking dish. Scatter blueberries over the bread and sprinkle evenly with crumb mixture. Bake about 40 minutes, or until golden brown. Before serving, top with strawberries.

Favorite Christmas morning breakfast

Marcia Swain
Key Largo Florida • Florida Keys Electric Cooperative

Spicy Peanut Chicken

1 lb. fresh chicken, boneless and skinless, cut into 1-inch pieces
½ medium red bell pepper, diced
¼ c. onion, chopped
1 tsp. minced garlic (fresh or bottled)
¾ c. mango/peach salsa
1 heaping Tbsp. chunky peanut butter
1 Tbsp. light soy sauce
1 Tbsp. balsamic vinegar
1 tsp. ground ginger
1 tsp. ground cumin
½ to ¾ c. water

Spray a large skillet with vegetable oil cooking spray and warm over medium-high heat. Brown chicken in skillet until golden brown, about 4 minutes. Add bell pepper, onion and garlic; sauté 1 to 2 minutes. Add salsa, peanut butter, soy sauce, vinegar, ginger, cumin and water. Stir together and cook over medium heat for approximately 4 minutes. Serve over rice.

Kay Hollo
Union, Oregon • Oregon Trail Electric Cooperative

Macadamia-Crusted Pear Torte

Crust:
1½ c. flour
½ c. butter, softened
1½ c. sugar
1½ c. macadamia nuts, chopped

Filling:
8 oz. soft cream cheese
¼ c. sugar
1 egg
1 tsp. vanilla
1 ripe pear, peeled and sliced
1½ tsp. cinnamon
½ tsp. nutmeg
1 tsp. lemon juice
¼ c. sugar

To make crust, combine ingredients in a bowl and mix well. Press onto bottom and sides of an 8-inch tart pan. Bake at 350 degrees for 12 minutes, or until crust begins to brown. Set aside to cool.

Increase oven temperature to 400 degrees.

To make filling, combine cream cheese, sugar, egg and vanilla in a bowl and mix well. Pour into the prepared tart pan over crust. Combine pears, cinnamon, nutmeg, lemon juice and ¼ c. sugar in a bowl. Toss to coat the pears. Arrange the pears in a circle over the cream cheese filling, including all liquid.

Bake for 20 to 25 minutes, or until set.

Joyce Miller
Coolin, Idaho • Northern Lights

Cranberry Salsa

1 bag fresh cranberries, coarsely chopped
1 handful cilantro, chopped
1 bunch green onions, chopped
½ to ¾ c. sugar
2 to 3 jalapeno peppers, minced (use as many or few peppers as you like until you get it to the heat you want)

Coarsely chop cranberries in a food processor. Do not chop too fine or purée. Add cilantro and peppers. Process for a few seconds, long enough to blend.

Pour into bowl and add green onions and sugar. Mix well, then cover and refrigerate. Let sit for at least an hour or so, long enough for the sugar to dissolve and meld into the cranberries.

Serve with crackers and a block of cream cheese.

Claudia Milazzo
Brookings, Oregon • Coos-Curry Electric Cooperative

Ponche Mexicano

2 gal. water
4 apples, cut into four pieces
4 cinnamon sticks
1 piloncillo or 1 c. brown sugar
½ lb. tejocotes
3 to 4 tamarindos
1 lb. guavas (fresh or canned)
About a foot-long piece of fresh-peeled sugar cane (from a jar is fine)

All of the ingredients are available at your local Mexican store.

Wash all of the fruit and slice into pieces. In a large pot, bring all of the ingredients to boil until the fruit is soft. This takes about 15 minutes. Serve warm. You can add tequila or rum at serving time.

One of the things I look forward to at Christmas is a drink called Ponche Mexicano—a delicious hot fruity drink. Ponche is very popular in Mexico at the posadas, but is quickly becoming pretty popular in the United States because of its unique blend of fruits and spices. My mother says this drink is as popular as eggnog, but better because it can easily turn into a cocktail drink by just adding tequila or rum.

Briselda Molina
Veneta, Oregon • Lane Electric

Cottage Cheese Dip

1 container cottage cheese
2 avocados, diced
½ red onion, diced
½ tsp. garlic powder
1 Tbsp. mayonnaise
Salt and pepper, to taste

Mix all ingredients in a bowl. Serve with chips and veggies.

This has been in the family over 40 years. It always gets good reviews.

Terry Lee Conlan
Bend, Oregon • Central Oregon Electric Cooperative

Stuffed Portobello Mushrooms

Portobello mushrooms, one per person
Eggs, beaten (usually one per large portobello)
Bread crumbs combined with grated Parmesan cheese
Soft Monterey Jack cheese or mozzarella (your choice)
Red sauce
Oil
Parmesan cheese, grated

Preheat oven to 350 degrees.

Remove the stem of the mushroom and set aside. With a sharp knife, gently peel the skin off the top of the portobello. Discard skin.

Dip mushroom in beaten egg until well covered. Place bread-crumb mixture in a plastic bag and gently roll the mushroom until it is totally covered.

Place in a heated frying pan with oil on low. Fry until lightly browned on both sides.

In a baking dish, place the mushroom underneath side up. Take a tablespoon of red sauce and spread in portobello center. Place several pieces of cheese, covering the entire mushroom. Then pour red sauce, engulfing over all.

Cover with foil and bake approximately 25 minutes. When cooked, remove from oven and let rest for 5 minutes. Remove foil and sprinkle with Parmesan cheese and serve hot.

Stems can be sliced or chopped, fried in butter and frozen. They can be thawed, warmed and used later to spread over a steak, or saved to use when making your own red sauce.

This is my family's very favorite way to eat portobellos.

Aurora Leveroni
Graeagle, California • Plumas-Sierra Rural Electric Cooperative

Tortilla Roll-Ups

12 oz. Italian sausage or hamburger
1 c. cream-style cottage cheese
1 Tbsp. flour
½ tsp. dried oregano, crushed
½ tsp. dried basil, crushed
1/8 tsp. garlic powder
15½-oz. jar spaghetti sauce (if you use zesty spaghetti
    sauce, omit oregano, basil and garlic)
8 flour tortillas
¼ c. mozzarella cheese, shredded

In a skillet, cook the sausage until browned; drain off fat. Stir in cottage cheese and flour. Add oregano, basil and garlic powder to the spaghetti sauce. Stir ½ c. spaghetti sauce into the sausage mixture. Cook and stir until mixture bubbles.

Spoon about ⅓ c. meat mixture onto each tortilla; roll up jelly-roll style. Place filled tortillas, seam side down, in a 12-by-17-inch baking pan. Pour remaining spaghetti sauce over tortillas. Bake, covered, in a 350-degree oven for 30 to 35 minutes.

Uncover and sprinkle mozzarella cheese on top. Bake 3 more minutes, or until cheese melts.

Brenda Burdick
Spring Creek, Nevada • Wells Rural Electric

Appetizers and Snacks

Alaska Crab Spread

3 Tbsp. warm water
1 envelope Knox gelatin
1 can cream of mushroom soup
8 oz. cream cheese
1 c. mayonnaise
1 c. celery, chopped
¼ c. red pepper, chopped
¼ c. lemon juice
3 Tbsp. onion, grated
2 to 3 cans crab, drained
Parsley sprigs for garnish

Mix warm water and gelatin, stirring to dissolve. Set aside.

In a saucepan, warm soup and cream cheese, stirring constantly. Add gelatin mixture to this, and mix well.

Stir in all other ingredients, except for crab. When well mixed, remove from heat and fold in drained crab meat.

Pour into a one-quart mold or springform pan. Refrigerate overnight.

Unmold and garnish with fresh parsley. Serve with crackers of your choice.

Joyce Miller
Coolin, Idaho • Northern Lights

Artichoke and Parmesan Dip

3 jars marinated artichoke hearts
3-oz. can mild green chilies
1 c. Parmesan cheese
½ c. mayonnaise

Drain artichoke hearts and pulse in food processor until coarsely chopped. Combine chopped artichoke hearts with remaining ingredients and scoop into a pie pan.

Bake at 350 degrees for 20 to 30 minutes until bubbling and cooked through. Serve with crackers or sliced vegetables.

This recipe is a favorite to take to potlucks. I sometimes just make it at home so everyone can enjoy, as there are never any leftovers!

Trina Harris
Sandpoint, Idaho • Northern Lights

Bacon-Wrapped Water Chestnuts in Special Sauce

2 lbs. bacon (approximately)
3 5-oz. cans whole water chestnuts
Small amount of garlic salt
Sauce:
1 c. ketchup
1 c. brown sugar
1 small can crushed pineapple
2 to 3 Tbsp. white wine or rice vinegar
½ tsp. ground ginger
1 tsp. cornstarch, dissolved in small amount of cold water

To make sauce, combine first five ingredients in a bowl until sugar is dissolved. Add cornstarch and stir until slightly thickened. Set aside.

Preheat oven to 350 degrees.

Cut bacon slices in half. Partially cook bacon in skillet until three-fourths done. Remove from skillet and place on paper towel. Drain water chestnuts. Wrap each one with a piece of bacon and secure with a toothpick.

Place wrapped water chestnuts on cookie sheet and bake for 20 minutes. Remove from oven and pour sauce over water chestnuts. Sprinkle with garlic salt and bake for an additional 15 minutes in sauce.

This recipe was passed on to me from my father. Always our family's favorite appetizer.

George Miller
Goldendale, Washington • Klickitat PUD

Bay's Buffalo Chicken Dip

8 oz. cream cheese, softened
½ c. ranch dressing
1 can chicken or 2 c. chicken breasts, cooked and shredded
1 c. Cheddar cheese
¼ to ½ c. red hot sauce
Preheat oven to 350 degrees.

Combine cream cheese and ranch dressing until smooth. Add chicken and mix well. Add red hot sauce to taste.

Place in oven-safe dish and heat for 20 minutes. Add cheese on top and bake until melted. Serve with tortilla chips.

Alma Osborne
Panama City, Florida • Gulf Coast Electric Cooperative

Bird Seed Snack Mix

2 boxes Ritz Bitz
1 box Corn Chex
2 bags pretzels
1 bag Cheddar fish
1 bag crunchy cheese curls
2 bags honey barbecue twists
1 bag corn chips
1 bag spicy corn chips
1 box Wheat Thins
1 lb. salted peanuts
1 lb. mixed nuts
1 bottle Orville Redenbacher popcorn oil
1 package ranch dressing (dry mix)

Mix together dry ingredients (everything except popcorn oil and ranch dressing). Mix popcorn oil and ranch and pour over salty mixture. Mix well.

This mix is good frozen as well.

Shayla Derstine
Canby, California • Surprise Valley Electrification

Corn Salsa

2 cans corn, drained
1 can black-eye peas, rinsed and drained
1 can black beans
1 bunch cilantro, chopped
1 bunch green onions, chopped
4 medium tomatoes, chopped
16-oz. bottle Italian salad dressing

Mix all ingredients together and refrigerate. Serve with corn chips.

Marci Larsen
Burley, Idaho • United Electric

Crab Bundles

2 Tbsp. salted butter
4 oz. cream cheese, softened
½ c. mozzarella cheese, shredded
½ c. Cheddar cheese, shredded
6 oz. crabmeat, picked over for shells and
    squeezed to remove excess moisture
2 cloves garlic
2 Tbsp. dried parsley flakes
½ tsp. lemon juice
2 Tbsp. green onions, chopped
2 8-oz. cans refrigerated crescent rolls

Preheat oven to 375 degrees. Lightly spray baking sheet with cooking spray. In a medium bowl, combine cream cheese, mozzarella, Cheddar, crabmeat, garlic, parsley flakes, salt and lemon juice. Set aside.

In a small skillet over medium-low heat, melt butter. Add green onions and sauté for 2 minutes. Add to crab mixture and stir to combine.

Unroll each tube of dough and separate into 8 triangles, totaling 16 triangles. Spoon about 1 Tbsp. of filling on wide end of each triangle.

Roll up each triangle, beginning with the wide end. Tuck ends under and place bundles on prepared baking sheet. Bake until golden brown, about 15 minutes.

Shar Lequerica
La Grande, Oregon • Oregon Trail Electric Cooperative

Crab Dip

8 oz. cream cheese
1 can cream of mushroom soup
1 c. celery, finely chopped
2 green or red onions, finely chopped
7-oz. can crab or 1 c. chopped imitation crab
1 c. Miracle Whip
Heat together the cream cheese and soup, and mix well. Add remaining ingredients. Mix all together and refrigerate overnight. Serve with crackers or chips.

Bonnie White
Baker City, Oregon • Oregon Trail Electric Cooperative

Cucumber Dip

2 8-oz. packages cream cheese
6 to 7 Tbsp. Miracle Whip
1 shredded cucumber, drained and peeled
4 Tbsp. onion, chopped
1 or more Tbsp. milk for desired consistency
Mix cream cheese and Miracle Whip, then add remaining ingredients. Let it sit overnight for best results.

After peeling the cucumber, drain it very well until you get almost no liquid from it. If you don't drain it well enough, the dip just doesn't taste right and will be watery.

I don't use level tablespoons of the Miracle Whip or onion, I just scoop and go. If I have leftover onion, I just throw it in, too.

Donna Lisk
Philomath, Oregon

Glazed Almonds

1 c. slivered almonds
1 tsp. vanilla
½ c. sugar
2 Tbsp. butter
Salt
In heavy skillet (nonstick doesn't work), place almonds, vanilla, sugar and butter. Stir over medium heat until caramelized.

Place on aluminum foil in 3 to 4 nut clusters. Salt lightly.

Note: You need to work quickly once the caramelization starts.

This is our holiday recipe that we've made for Thanksgiving, Christmas and New Year's since 1962/3. It's addictive, and it does not break teeth.

Jane Streek
Alpharetta, Georgia; and Goldendale, Washington • Klickitat PUD

Guacamole

2 avocados, mashed with potato masher until creamy
1 Tbsp. lemon juice
¼ tsp. chili powder
1 Tbsp. onion, finely diced
1 tsp. cilantro
Dash of garlic powder
A few grape tomatoes, chopped (or add
    your favorite salsa to taste)
⅓ c. mayonnaise
Mix all together and cover top with mayonnaise (enough to seal top).

Chill for 1 to 2 hours. Stir together and serve with chips.

Mickye Sheidler
Panama City, Florida • Gulf Coast Electric Cooperative

Healthy Snack

½ c. peanut butter
½ c. quick oatmeal
⅓ c. honey
½ c. dark chocolate chips
Mix ingredients together, then put in refrigerator for 30 minutes. Form into mini balls.

Received this from my grandson, as his wife likes to give them to their little boys instead of candy.

Adelia Olson
Norfolk, Nebraska • Elkhorn Rural Public Power

Marinated Chicken Wings

3 lbs. chicken wings
¼ c. soy sauce
½ c. brown sugar
1 Tbsp. water
2 Tbsp. honey
1 Tbsp. hoisin sauce

Clean chicken wings. Cut off tip and cut in two at joint.

Marinate overnight. Bake for 1½ hours, uncovered, at 325 degrees. Baste several times while baking.

We've served these during our Christmastime family gatherings for longer than I can remember. Always an added reason to go home for Christmas!

Lori Linville
La Pine, Oregon • Midstate Electric

Melody's Garlicious Spinach Dip for a Crowd

2 10-oz. packages frozen chopped spinach, thawed
   and drained in a colander in the sink with as much
   water as you can squeeze out with paper towels
8-oz. can sliced or whole water chestnuts,
   finely chopped (at least ½ c.)
1 small sweet onion, finely chopped (at least ½ c.)
6 to 8 cloves fresh garlic, finely chopped/minced
2 Tbsp. dry mustard (start with 1 Tbsp. and add to taste)
16 oz. light sour cream
1 c. mayonnaise
16 oz. light cream cheese (I use Western Family,
   surprisingly creamier flavor than Philly)
1 large sourdough bread round, at least 8 to 12 inches
   around and 5 to 7 inches tall, with top 2 to 3 inches cut
   off like a lid; tear out the middle of the round and save
   for stuffing or use for dipping after toasting first
Sea salt
Black pepper

In a large bowl, cream the mayo, cream cheese and sour cream. Add the vegetables and dry mustard and at least 1 tsp. salt and ¼ tsp. pepper. Mix well and add more garlic if you like.

Put mixed spinach dip in the bread bowl with the topper and wrap it in plastic wrap tightly in the fridge for at least 1 to 2 hours. If there is extra, be sure it's in a plastic container with a tight-fitting lid, and store in the fridge.

Serve with crackers, toasted bread pieces and veggies on a large platter with the dip bowl in the middle. Be sure to refrigerate leftovers. Don't leave dip out for more than two hours, or put it on a chilled platter.

Everyone who tries this dip wants the recipe.

Melody Wagoner
Goldendale, Washington • Klickitat PUD

Paté

½ lb. Braunschweiger, at room temperature
2 Tbsp. mayonnaise
2 tsp. sweet pickle relish
4 oz. cream cheese, at room temperature
1 hard-boiled egg, chopped
2 Tbsp. onion, finely chopped
½ tsp. Worcestershire sauce
1 tsp. Dijon mustard

Put all ingredients in large bowl. Mix with electric mixer until blended. Chill. Serve with assorted crackers. May be frozen.

Shirley J. Tumbush
Panama City, Florida

Salmon Ceviche Ole!

½ lb. raw salmon, chopped
3 large tomatoes (3 c. worth), chopped
1 clove garlic, chopped fine
1 c. onion, chopped
½ c. fresh cilantro, chopped
2 serano peppers, gutted and chopped fine (seeds may
   be left in or peppers may be omitted from recipe)
¾ c. lime juice
1 tsp. salt

Mix all ingredients in a large mixing bowl. Transfer into a large jar, cover and refrigerate overnight. Acid from the lime juice will fully cook the salmon.

Serve in a bowl as a dip for tortilla chips or crackers.

Variation: Drain lime juice from mix after overnight refrigeration and mix in 8 oz. of room-temperature cream cheese for a savory dip.

Cylle Pompa
North Pole, Alaska

Salmon or Crab Mousse

One envelope unflavored gelatin
¼ c. boiling water
3 Tbsp. lemon juice
6-oz. can salmon, drained
¾ c. mayonnaise
½ tsp. dill
Dash of salt
Dash of pepper
½ c. celery, chopped

Blend gelatin, water and lemon juice. Add remaining ingredients and blend just until all ingredients are combined.

Spray a gelatin mold pan with nonstick spray. Pour in mousse and refrigerate until firm. Unmold and serve with small bread slices or crackers.

Charlotte Robson
Bradenton, Florida • Peace River Electric Cooperative

Sausage and Cream Cheese Dip

1 lb. Jimmy Dean hot sausage
8-oz. brick cream cheese
1 can Rotel diced tomatoes, regular, undrained
Brown sausage in a pan. Add cream cheese and tomatoes. Heat until smooth. Serve warm with tortilla chips or on toasted French bread slices.

This is a recipe that I get asked to share every time I serve or bring it somewhere.

Myrna Bessler
Coolidge, Arizona

Vegetable Bars

2 tubes crescent rolls
¾ c. mayonnaise
½ c. sour cream
2 8-oz. packages cream cheese
1 package ranch dressing mix
¾ c. green pepper, chopped
¾ c. green onion, chopped
¾ c. tomato, diced
¾ c. broccoli, chopped
¾ c. carrots, shredded
¾ c. cauliflower, chopped
¾ c. Cheddar cheese, shredded
Pat and stretch crescent rolls over 11-by-17-inch cookie sheet. Bake at 350 degrees for 7 to 10 minutes.

Mix mayonnaise, sour cream, cream cheese and ranch dressing mix. Spread mixture evenly over cooled crust.

Mix together all vegetables and pack onto creamed mixture. Top with cheese.

Refrigerate for 3 to 4 hours and slice into squares.

Margaret Nichols
Baker City, Oregon

Breads, Buns, Rolls, Waffles, Pancakes

Banana Bread

½ c. butter
1 c. sugar (or Splenda)
3 medium bananas
2 eggs
2 c. flour
½ tsp. salt
1 tsp. soda
1 tsp. baking powder
1 tsp. vanilla
Raisins, nuts or dried fruit (optional)
Cream butter, vanilla and sugar. Add flour and bananas alternately. Bake at 350 degrees until top is brown.

This recipe was used in 1936 by the mother of a good friend of mine.

Carol Huber
Oakridge, Oregon • Lane Electric

Banana Bread

3 c. flour
2 c. sugar
1 tsp. baking soda
2 tsp. pumpkin pie spice
3 eggs
¾ c. margarine or butter
3 bananas, mashed
2 tsp. almond extract
8-oz. can crushed pineapple, undrained
Brown sugar
Beat softened margarine or butter. Add eggs until light and fluffy. Add mashed bananas and crushed pineapple. Add flour mixture on low speed for a couple minutes, then medium speed for 2 to 3 minutes. Pour into greased and floured loaf pans. Top each loaf with a generous sprinkling of brown sugar.

Bake at 350 degrees for 55 to 60 minutes for a large loaf pan, or 35 to 40 minutes if you use small loaf pans. The recipe makes four small loaf pans.

Arleen Rice
Walla Walla, Washington • Columbia REA

Banana Nut Applesauce Loaf

2½ c. sugar
3 eggs
3 c. flour, sifted
3 tsp. vanilla
1 c. oil
2 c. banana, smashed
1 c. cinnamon applesauce
¼ tsp. salt
1 tsp. baking soda
¼ tsp. baking powder
1 c. nuts
3 tsp. cinnamon
Preheat oven to 350 degrees.

Combine all ingredients. Pour into two greased loaf pans. Bake for one hour and 15 minutes. Let cool.

John Wicker
Mesa, Arizona

Best-Ever Banana Bread

3 Tbsp. butter or margarine
1 c. sugar
2 eggs
3 Tbsp. buttermilk
3 ripe bananas, sliced
2 c. flour
1 tsp. baking soda
1 tsp. salt
1 to 2 tsp. vanilla
Place all ingredients into a food processor and mix thoroughly. Bake in a loaf pan at 350 degrees for 1 hour or until toothpick test shows the bread is done. If using two small loaf pans, bake for 45 minutes.

If using a mixing bowl and electric mixer, cream shortening and sugar together. Add eggs and beat well. Add buttermilk, bananas and vanilla; beat. Add flour, baking soda and salt; beat. Spoon batter into a loaf pan.

This recipe has been in our family for three generations and is the best we have ever tasted.

Rosemary Soper
Bellevue, Washington, and Manzanita, Oregon • Tillamook PUD

Caramel Rolls

2 c. hot water
¼ c. oil
¼ c. sugar
2 heaping Tbsp. yeast
1½ tsp. salt
4 c. flour (may need additional)
½ c. butter
½ c. brown sugar
½ tsp. cinnamon
Caramel:
1 c. whipping cream
1 c. brown sugar
2 to 3 Tbsp. butter
1 tsp. vanilla

Place water, oil, sugar, yeast, salt and flour in mixer and beat until dough comes away from the sides of the dish. Let rise until double.

Roll out half of the dough at a time. Spread same amounts of butter, brown sugar and cinnamon on dough. Roll up and cut about 2-inch size for rolls.

While dough is rising, make caramel. In a saucepan, simmer whipping cream and brown sugar. If you like it thick, simmer longer. Then add butter and vanilla. Cool.

Pour sauce into a 9-by-13-inch pan. Place rolls on cool caramel sauce. Let rise until double.

Bake at 350 degrees for 25 minutes.

This recipe also makes two loaves of bread or one loaf with a 9-by-9-inch pan of rolls.

Marlene Hostetler
Springfield, Oregon

Cranberry Orange Bread

2 c. whole wheat flour or barley flour
¾ c. sugar
1½ tsp. baking powder
½ tsp. baking soda
½ tsp. salt
¼ c. butter, softened
1 Tbsp. grated orange peel
¾ c. orange juice
1 orange, chopped, seeds removed
1 egg
1 c. frozen or fresh cranberries
1 c. pecans or walnuts
Preheat oven to 400 degrees. Mix all ingredients together and spread in a greased loaf pan.

Bake for 50 to 60 minutes, then check with toothpick.

Teri Hruska
Fairbanks, Alaska • Golden Valley Electric Association

Creamy Cinnamon Rolls

1 loaf frozen bread dough, thawed
2 Tbsp. butter, melted
⅔ c. brown sugar
½ c. chopped nuts and raisins, optional
1 tsp. cinnamon
½ to ⅔ c. heavy cream (do not whip)
Glaze:
⅔ c. powdered sugar
1 Tbsp. milk or cream
1 Tbsp. softened butter
½ tsp. vanilla

Grease two round baking pans or a 9-by-13-inch pan. Preheat oven to 350 degrees.

Roll dough to an 18-by-6-inch rectangle. Brush with the melted butter. Combine brown sugar, nuts and cinnamon; sprinkle evenly over dough. Roll in jelly-roll fashion. Moisten edges and seal. Cut into approximately 20 slices.

Place rolls, cut side down, in the prepared pans. Let rise until doubled, about 1½ hours. Pour the cream over the rolls. Bake for 25 minutes. Mix the powdered sugar, milk, butter and vanilla until smooth. While the rolls are warm, drizzle with glaze.

Janet Spriet
Baker City, Oregon • Oregon Trail Electric Cooperative

Grandma Vi's Zucchini Bread

3 eggs
1 c. oil
2 c. sugar
2 c. zucchini, grated
3 tsp. vanilla
2 c. flour
1 tsp. salt
1 tsp. baking soda
3 tsp. cinnamon
¼ tsp. baking powder

Preheat oven to 350 degrees.

Beat eggs until foamy. Add oil, sugar, zucchini and vanilla. Mix well. Add flour and other dry ingredients. Mix well.

Bake in two well-greased loaf pans or one well-greased Bundt pan for 1 hour.

Cool in pan on wire rack for 10 minutes. Remove from pan and cool completely.

This is a family recipe from my 91-year-old mother-in-law.

Trina Smith
Noti, Oregon • Blachly-Lane Electric Cooperative

Granny's Banana Bread

2 bananas
2 eggs
2 heaping Tbsp. shortening
1 c. sugar
Dash of salt
1½ c. all-purpose flour
1 tsp. baking soda
Nuts (optional)

Mix bananas, eggs and shortening in blender (or blend by hand). Add sugar, salt, flour, baking soda and nuts.

Bake in a loaf pan for 1 hour at 325 degrees.

Wende Blackburn
Lake Wales, Florida

Mom's Cinnamon Pull-a-Parts

2 c. milk
½ c. sugar
2 eggs, beaten
¼ c. shortening, melted
2 yeast cakes, dissolved in ¼ c. lukewarm water
3 tsp. salt
6 to 7 c. flour
Mixture:
1½ c. sugar
2 tsp. cinnamon
½ c. nuts, chopped
Butter, melted

Scald milk and mix together sugar, eggs and shortening. Add milk and let cool to lukewarm. Add yeast, then add flour mixture until dough is of a consistency to clean bowl. Knead and let rise for 1 to 2 hours.

Cut dough into 1-inch balls, roll in butter and then roll in mixture. Layer the balls in an angel food cake tin or Bundt pan. Let rise for 30 minutes in 350-degree oven. (I like to set a piece of tin foil on top, but not tightened, to keep the top from getting crunchy.)

These can be made in advance. As soon as they are layered, cover and put in the freezer. Let thaw on the counter the night before you use them.

Every year on Christmas Eve, the last thing my mom did before going to bed was make cinnamon pull-a-parts. She would put them in the fridge and then the first thing on Christmas morning, she'd pull them out and pop them in the oven while we were opening the gifts. It was the only time of the year that she made them. I began making them for other special occasions and always when there was a bunch of family together. Now, the granddaughters are making them.

Tracy Blais
Delta Junction, Alaska • Golden Valley Electric Association

Mom's Cinnamon Rolls

2 Tbsp. yeast
½ c. warm water
2 c. lukewarm milk
½ c. sugar
½ c. vegetable oil
1 tsp. baking powder
2 tsp. salt
1 egg
¼ tsp. nutmeg
5 to 6 c. flour
Filling:
2 c. brown sugar
1 c. butter (no substitutes)
2 tsp. cinnamon
Nuts, optional

Dissolve yeast in warm water. Stir in milk, sugar, oil, baking powder, salt, egg, nutmeg and 2 to 3 cups of flour. Beat until smooth. Add enough remaining flour to make dough easy to handle. Knead until smooth. Let rise until double (about an hour).

Grease two 9-by-13-inch pans. Divide dough in half and roll into 12-by-10-inch rectangle for each half.

Heat brown sugar and butter until melted. Remove from heat and stir in cinnamon. Spread over each half of dough and sprinkle with nuts, if desired. Roll and slice. Place in greased pans and wrap tightly with foil. Refrigerate at least 12 hours and not more than 48 hours.

To bake, remove foil. Bake at 350 degrees for 30 to 35 minutes.

May also let rise after placing in pan and bake without refrigeration. This recipe also does well in a Dutch oven for camping purposes.

Candace Zaugg
Tillamook, Oregon • Tillamook PUD

Morning Glory Muffins

1¼ c. granulated sugar
½ c. vegetable oil
3 eggs
2 tsp. vanilla
2 c. all-purpose flour
2 tsp. baking powder
¼ tsp. salt
1 tsp. cinnamon
2 c. carrots, grated
½ c. raisins
½ c. coconut
½ c. apple, peeled and diced
½ c. pecans, chopped

Preheat oven to 350 degrees.

Combine sugar, oil, eggs and vanilla in a large bowl. Combine flour, baking powder, salt and cinnamon in another bowl. Add to the liquid ingredients and stir until just moistened. Gently fold in remaining ingredients.

Pour into well-greased muffin tins to about two-thirds full. Bake 20 to 25 minutes.

Jill Luoma
Marathon, Florida

Oven French Toast

12-oz. loaf of French bread, cut into 1½-inch slices (14 pieces)
2 c. milk
½ tsp. nutmeg
8 large eggs
2 c. half-and-half
½ tsp. cinnamon
Topping:
¾ c. butter
3 Tbsp. dark Karo syrup
1½ c. brown sugar
1⅓ c. chopped nuts

Place bread in heavily buttered 9-by-13-inch pan; set aside. In a mixing bowl, beat eggs; add milk, nutmeg, half-and-half, vanilla and cinnamon. Pour over bread. Cover and refrigerate overnight.

Before baking, make the topping. Spread over the bread mixture.

Bake at 350 degrees for about 50 minutes.

This is a tried-and-true recipe that is enjoyed at my brunches.

Geraldine Boswell
Lacon, Illinois

Poppy Seed Bread

4 eggs
2 c. sugar
1½ c. oil
3 c. flour
1½ tsp. baking soda
½ tsp. salt
1 can milk
2 oz. poppy seeds

Beat eggs until thick. Gradually beat in the sugar. Stir in oil.

Mix flour, soda and salt together. Stir in one-third of the dry ingredients, then half a can of milk. Continue until all are well mixed. Add poppy seeds.

Pour into a 10-inch ungreased tube pan, and bake at 350 degrees for 1 hour and 10 minutes.

Cool completely before turning out of pan. Some like to spread slices with cream cheese or butter. Others like it plain.

This has been a favorite family recipe for 40 years. It has been the champion baked good exhibit at our local county fair, and the Oregon State Fair. No branding party would be complete without it.

Sharon Livingston
Long Creek, Oregon • Oregon Trail Electric Cooperative

Pumpkin Nut Applesauce Loaf

2½ c. sugar
3 eggs
3 c. flour, sifted
3 tsp. vanilla
1 c. oil
2 c. pumpkin
1 c. cinnamon applesauce
¼ tsp. salt
1 tsp. baking soda
¼ tsp. baking powder
1 c. nuts
3 tsp. allspice
Preheat oven to 350 degrees.

Combine all ingredients. Pour into two greased loaf pans. Bake for one hour and 15 minutes. Let cool.

John Wicker
Mesa, Arizona

Quick Bread Sticks

½ c. butter
2¼ c. flour
½ tsp. seasoning salt
1 Tbsp. sugar
3½ tsp. baking powder
2 Tbsp. Parmesan cheese
½ tsp. powdered garlic
1 c. milk
Celery salt (optional)
While heating the oven to 450 degrees, melt butter in a 9-by-13-inch pan.

In a bowl, mix flour, seasoning salt, sugar, baking powder, Parmesan cheese and powdered garlic.

Add milk to mixture.

Mix together and turn out on floured board. Knead approximately 10 times. Roll ½-inch thick. Cut into strips—a pizza cutter works best to do this. Roll each strip in the melted butter and give it a twist. Place strips close together in the pan. Before baking, you may sprinkle the strips with garlic or celery salt and/or Parmesan cheese.

Bake for 15 minutes.

Kay Hollo
Vancouver, Washington, and Union, Oregon • Oregon Trail Electric Cooperative

Rhubarb Buns

Dough:
8 or 9 c. flour
½ c. sugar
1 Tbsp. salt
2 Tbsp. yeast
¾ c. oil
3 c. lukewarm water, or 1½ c. milk and 1½ c. water
3 eggs
Cinnamon sugar mixture:
1 c. white sugar
½ tsp. cinnamon
Rhubarb mixture:
3 c. rhubarb, cut in very small pieces
1 c. sugar
½ tsp. cinnamon

Mix all dough ingredients together and knead either by machine or hand for 7 minutes. Place in greased bowl and cover. Let rise for 1 hour, punching down every 20 minutes. Shape into buns. Roll in cinnamon and sugar mixture.

Space 2 inches apart on greased cookie sheets. Let rise 10 to 15 minutes. Punch a hole in the center using a 1-inch salt shaker and fill immediately with 1 tsp. of the rhubarb mixture.

Let rise until double, two hours or so. Bake at 350 degrees for 20 minutes.

Each spring, when the rhubarb was ready to pick, my great-grandmother would make these for her family. We like them as much as they did, and have continued the tradition.

Rachel Giesbrecht
Othello, Washington • Big Bend Electric

Sourdough Waffles

1 c. sourdough starter (see recipe below)
½ c. oats
½ c. wheat flour
1 c. white flour
1 to 2 c. water
2 eggs
1 Tbsp. sugar
2 tsp. baking soda

In a glass bowl, combine sourdough starter, oats and flours, adding water when mixture gets too thick. Mixture should resemble cake batter. Cover with a tea towel and let sit overnight.

In the morning, while the waffle iron is heating, add eggs, sugar, baking soda and water, if needed. Beat with fork until batter has risen. Pour immediately.

Sourdough starter:

1 c. unbleached flour
1 c. water, at room temperature
3 rounded tsp. sugar

Combine water, sugar and flour. Beat with a whisk until well blended. Pour into a wide-mouth jar large enough for starter to expand. Let stand, covered lightly, in a warm place for 2 to 3 days, until the mixture is bubbly. Mix with a fork, beating slightly every day.

After sourdough is used, replenish with additional flour.

I made these wonderful waffles for my kids, cousins, aunt and mother and they helped me create a beautiful walkway to my house. After fueling up on buttery warm waffles topped with fresh berries and cream, we had a great time building the walkway with shells, marbles and pottery. After several waffle parties there was a "walkway to the waffles."

Nancy King
Delta Junction, Alaska • Golden Valley Electric Association

Swedish Pancakes

3 c. flour
2 Tbsp. sugar
1 tsp. baking powder
1 tsp. salt
4 c. milk
4 eggs
1 tsp. vanilla
4 Tbsp. butter, melted

Measure flour, sugar, baking powder and salt into large bowl. Stir in remaining ingredients. Beat with a rotary or electric beater until smooth.

For each pancake, lightly oil an 8-inch skillet; heat over medium heat until butter is bubbly. Pour ¼ c. of the batter into skillet. Immediately rotate pan until batter covers bottom. Cook until light brown; turn and brown on other side.

To serve, spoon on applesauce, sour cream and strawberry jam, maple syrup or powdered sugar. The sky is the limit. You can also serve at supper and make savory sauces, i.e., cheese and broccoli sauce, fried mushrooms and chopped ham, etc. Once the choice of topping is made, roll up pancake and eat.

Ruth Keller
Redmond, Oregon • Central Electric Cooperative

Desserts: Bars

Filled Dream Bars

1 box pound cake mix
4 eggs
1 stick butter
1 lb. powdered sugar
1 c. pecans
8 oz. cream cheese

Combine pound cake mix, 2 eggs and butter. Spread in a 9-by-13-inch pan.

Combine powdered sugar, pecans, cream cheese and 2 eggs. Pour over cake mix.

Bake at 350 degrees for 35 to 40 minutes. Sprinkle with powdered sugar.

Shirley Glessner
Wauchula, Florida • Peace River Electric Cooperative

Homemade Granola Bars

4½ c. Rice Krispies
2 c. rolled oats
½ c. graham crackers, crushed
½ c. chocolate chips
½ c. butter
¼ c. vegetable oil
¼ c. honey
¾ c. peanut butter
1 lb. miniature marshmallows

In a large mixing bowl, stir together Rice Krispies, rolled oats, graham crackers and chocolate chips. Set aside.

In a large saucepan over low heat, melt together the butter, vegetable oil, honey, peanut butter and marshmallows. When marshmallows are completely melted, pour over dry mixture and quickly mix everything together with a strong mixing spoon. Keep mixing until chocolate chips are melted and everything is thoroughly combined.

Pour the mixture into a 9-by-13-inch Tupperware pan. Gently arrange it into the container. The secret is do not pack it down, just very gently fix it into the pan. Put on the lid tight right away. Cut it whenever you desire.

When we found this recipe, it was a winner. They are not so dense and packed as most other granola bars. They never last long at our house.

Malinda Schrock
Litchfield, California • Plumas-Sierra Rural Electric Cooperative

Krispy Kritters

½ c. margarine
16-oz. bag miniature marshmallows
1 c. butterscotch chips
6 c. Multigrain Cheerios
4 c. Rice Krispies
2 c. Lucky Charms

Melt margarine in large microwavable bowl. Add marshmallows. Stir and microwave for 90 seconds. Stir and repeat. Add butterscotch chips and stir well.

Add Cheerios, Rice Krispies and Lucky Charms. Stir until well coated.

Pour into buttered 9-by-13-inch baking dish. Press lightly. Let cool, then cut.

Juanita McCarl
Junction City, Oregon

Rice Krispies Bars

1 c. peanut butter
1 c. sugar
1 c. light corn syrup
6 c. Rice Krispies
1 c. chocolate chips
1 c. butterscotch chips

Melt and stir together peanut butter, sugar and corn syrup. Pour over Rice Krispies. Pat into a greased 9-by-13-inch pan.

Melt chocolate chips and butterscotch chips. Spread quickly over bars.

Carla Smith
Benton City, Washington • Benton REA

Salty Pretzel Bottom Blondies

3 c. pretzel twists
1 c. butter, at room temperature
1½ c. dark brown sugar
2 eggs
2 tsp. vanilla
2½ c. all-purpose flour
1 tsp. baking soda
1 tsp. coarse sea salt
3 c. coarsely chopped Snickers bars or unchopped Snickers Minis

Preheat oven to 350 degrees.

Spray a 9-by-13-inch pan with cooking spray. Line bottom of the pan with pretzels. In a stand mixer, cream butter and sugar together for 1 minute. Add in eggs and vanilla. Continue mixing for another minute, until smooth. Turn mixer to low and add in baking soda, salt and flour. Stir until just combined.

Add Snickers and turn up mixer to medium. Mix for 20 seconds until evenly incorporated and slightly broken up. Spread batter evenly over pretzels.

Bake for 30 to 35 minutes, until the center is almost set. Let cool completely. Cut into squares when ready to serve.

Donna Beck
Bonney Lake, Washington • Puget Sound Energy

Scotch Treats

6 oz. butterscotch chips
⅔ c. peanut butter
3 c. Rice Krispies

Place butterscotch chips and peanut butter in top of double boiler until melted. Remove from heat, stir and pour over cereal until well coated.

Press into a buttered 9-by-9-inch pan. Let stand until cooled.

Jo Tarver
Corvallis, Oregon • Consumers Power

Sour Cream Raisin Bars

2 c. raisins
¾ c. water
1 c. brown sugar
1 c. butter or softened oleo
1¾ c. flour
1 tsp. baking soda
1¾ c. oatmeal
3 egg yolks
1 c. sour cream
1 c. buttermilk
1 c. sugar
4 Tbsp. cornstarch
1 Tbsp. vanilla

Cook raisins in water for 5 minutes; set aside. Cream sugar and butter. Mix flour, baking soda and oatmeal. Add to sugar and butter mixture. Pour half of crumbs into a 9-by-13-inch cake pan. Bake at 325 for 7 minutes.

Mix egg yolks, sour cream, buttermilk, sugar and cornstarch. Cook on medium heat, stirring constantly, until boiling and thickened. Add raisins and vanilla.

Pour over baked crust. Top with remaining crumbs. Bake at 300 degrees for 30 minutes.

These bars are irresistible at our house.
Kathy Schrock
Litchfield, California • Plumas-Sierra Rural Electric Cooperative

Tom's Persimmon Bars

1 c. persimmon pulp (see below)
1 tsp. baking soda
1 egg
1 c. sugar
½ c. oil
8 oz. pitted dates, finely chopped
1¾ c. flour
1 tsp. salt
1 tsp. cinnamon
1 tsp. nutmeg
¼ tsp. ground cloves
1 c. walnuts or pecans, chopped

Cut three to four persimmons in half when they are very soft to the touch. Scoop out pulp. Chop up and add baking soda. Combine and set aside.

Beat eggs and sugar. Add oil and dates.

Combine all remaining dry ingredients. Add date mixture with pulp and stir in nuts.

Use a jelly roll pan (a cookie sheet with sides). Spray with cooking spray and spread mixture on pan. Bake at 350 degrees for 25 minutes. Cool for 5 minutes.

Lemon glaze:
1 c. powdered sugar
1 tsp. lemon juice

To make the glaze, mix powdered sugar and lemon juice. Spread the glaze after the bars have cooled for 5 minutes.

Thomas S. Koskey
Pahrump, Nevada • Valley Electric Association

Desserts: Cake

Baby Food Cake

2 c. self-rising flour
2 c. sugar
1 c. cooking oil
3 eggs
2 small jars apple blueberry baby food
¼ tsp. ground cloves
1 tsp. cinnamon
1 tsp. vanilla
1 c. pecans, chopped

Preheat oven to 350 degrees. Sift all dry ingredients together. Add oil, eggs, baby food, vanilla and pecans. Beat until well blended.

Pour into a nonstick coated Bundt pan and bake for 40 to 45 minutes. Cool and serve.

Hazel Wilson
Molino, Florida • Escambia River Electric Cooperative

Best Carrot Cake

3 c. shredded carrots
2 c. all-purpose flour
¾ c. granulated sugar
¾ c. brown sugar, firmly packed
2 tsp. baking powder
1 tsp. salt
2 tsp. baking soda
1 tsp. cinnamon
¼ tsp. cloves
¼ tsp. ginger
1 Tbsp. flax seed or meal (optional)
4 eggs
1¼ c. vegetable oil
1 c. walnuts or pecans, chopped
1 c. raisins

Cream cheese frosting:

8 oz. cream cheese, at room temperature
½ c. butter, at room temperature
2 tsp. vanilla
1-lb. box powdered sugar
½ c. chopped walnuts or pecans (optional)

Preheat oven to 350 degrees. Generously grease and flour two round cake pans or one 9-by-12-inch baking pan.

In a large bowl, combine flour, sugars, baking powder, salt, baking soda, flax and spices. Beat in eggs, oil and carrots. Beat on low speed until blended. Add chopped nuts.

Pour into prepared baking pan(s). Bake 25 to 30 minutes, or until toothpick inserted in the center comes out clean. Cool in the pans on a rack for 10 minutes. If using round pans, turn out on to rack to cool completely.

To make the frosting, beat the cream cheese and butter until fluffy. Blend in vanilla. Gradually add powdered sugar. Beat until smooth and creamy. Spread on cake and sprinkle nuts on top, if desired.

Barbara Darland
Redmond, Oregon · Central Electric Cooperative

Blueberry Pineapple Crunch Cake

¾ c. butter, melted
1 large can crushed pineapple, plus juice
20-oz. can blueberry pie filling
1 package yellow cake mix
1 c. pecans

Put crushed pineapple plus juice in the bottom of a 9-by-13-inch greased pan.

Spread blueberry pie filling over the top of the pineapple. Sprinkle dry cake mix on top of the pie filling. Pour butter over the cake mix and sprinkle nuts on top.

Bake at 350 degrees for 35 to 40 minutes.

My family really loves it. It's a recipe that the kids can make and be so proud that they did it.

Carol Lemley
Grass Valley, Oregon

Caramel Apple Cheesecake

1 c. graham cracker crumbs
3 Tbsp. brown sugar
½ tsp. ground cinnamon
¼ c. butter, melted
2 Tbsp. pecans, finely chopped

Filling:

3 8-oz. packages cream cheese, softened
¾ c. sugar
3 eggs
1 tsp. vanilla extract

Topping:

2½ c. apples, peeled and chopped
1 Tbsp. lemon juice
¼ c. brown sugar
1 tsp. ground cinnamon
6 Tbsp. caramel ice cream topping, divided
2 Tbsp. chopped pecans

Whipped cream:

1 c. heavy whipping cream
2 Tbsp. powdered sugar
1 tsp. vanilla extract

Combine the first five ingredients; press onto the bottom of a lightly greased 9-inch springform pan. Bake at 350 degrees for 10 minutes; cool.

In a mixing bowl, beat cream cheese and sugar until smooth. Add eggs; beat on low just until combined. Stir in vanilla and pour over crust.

Toss apples with lemon juice, sugar and cinnamon; spoon over filling.

Place springform pan in a large rectangular baking pan filled with 2 inches of hot water. Place in a 350-degree oven and bake for 55 to 60 minutes, or until center is almost set.

Remove cheesecake from oven and water-filled pan. Cool on a wire rack for 20 minutes. Carefully run a knife around the edge of the pan to loosen. Drizzle with 4 Tbsp. caramel topping.

Cool for 1 hour. Refrigerate overnight.

Remove sides of pan. Whip cream on high until soft peaks form. Gently add sugar and vanilla and beat until combined. Just before serving, garnish cheesecake with whipped cream. Drizzle with remaining caramel and sprinkle with pecans.

Carrie Falotico
Lebanon, Oregon · Consumers Power

Caramel Syrup Cake

1 c. Crisco oil
1½ c. white sugar
3 eggs
2 c. all-purpose flour, sifted twice
1 c. buttermilk
1 c. prunes, cooked
1 c. nuts, chopped
1 tsp. baking soda
1 tsp. salt
1 tsp. allspice
1 tsp. cinnamon
1 tsp. nutmeg
1 tsp. vanilla
Caramel icing:
1 c. white sugar
½ c. buttermilk
1 tsp. baking soda
1 cube margarine
½ tsp. vanilla
1 Tbsp. Karo syrup

Blend sugar with oil. Add eggs one at a time. Sift dry ingredients. Blend in buttermilk, nuts and prunes. Bake in greased and floured 10-inch tube pan for 1 hour at 350 degrees. When cake is half baked, start to make the icing.

Slowly cook icing ingredients and stir until soft ball stage, about 20 minutes. Pour over cake. Ice at once.

Judy Kryder
Bend, Oregon

Chess Cakes

½ c. butter
3 oz. cream cheese
1 c. flour
1 tsp. ground cinnamon
1 Tbsp. milk

Mix ingredients well. Refrigerate for 30 minutes.

Roll chilled pastry on a floured cloth to ¼-inch thick. Cut into 24 3-inch rounds. Fit into greased muffin tins. Refrigerate while preparing filling.

Filling:
3 eggs, separated
¼ c. butter
1 c. brown sugar
1 tsp. vanilla
1 c. raisins
1 c. nuts, chopped

In a large mixing bowl, cream together butter and brown sugar.

In a small, deep bowl, beat three egg whites until stiff. Gently fold into the butter and brown sugar mixture.

Add three egg yolks and vanilla. Beat well. Fold in the raisins and nuts. Spoon one tablespoonful into each pastry-lined muffin tin.

Bake at 375 degrees for 10 minutes, then at 300 degrees for 15 to 20 minutes until light brown.

My mother-in-law, Ethel Schaefer, served these holiday dessert treats.

Lynne Schaefer
Sunriver, Oregon • Midstate Electric Cooperative

Chocolate Cranberry Whip Cream Cake

Chocolate cake mix
2 cans whole cranberry sauce
1 can whip cream

Follow package directions for cake mix. Bake using two 8-inch cake pans.

Cool, then cut cake into equal squares. Before serving, cut squares in half, like a layer cake.

Mix one can of cranberries with some of the whip cream. Layer center with this mixture. Put top piece of cake over mixture. Spoon other can of cranberries over the cake. Top with whip cream.

Roselia Snyder
Brookings, Oregon

Chocolate Fudge Cake

1½ c. sugar
2 eggs
2 c. flour
1 tsp. baking soda
1 tsp. salt
1 tsp. baking powder
1 tsp. vanilla
½ c. oil
1 c. water
½ c. butter
½ c. cocoa powder
½ c. sour cream
12 oz. chocolate chips

In a saucepan, combine water, oil, butter and cocoa. Heat over low heat until butter is melted. Stir to blend ingredients.

In a mixing bowl, stir together the flour, sugar, salt, soda and powder. Pour cocoa mixture in and stir well. Add eggs, sour cream, chocolate chips and vanilla and stir until blended. Pour batter into a 9-by-13-inch baking pan. Bake at 350 degrees for

30 to 40 minutes, or until tested done.

With the chocolate chips in the cake, there is no need for frosting.

My family and extended family love this cake for special occasions.

Michelle Stace
Terrebonne, Oregon • Central Electric Cooperative

Cornflake Huckleberry Cake

½ c. walnuts or pecans, chopped
4 c. corn flakes, crushed to 1⅓ c.
1 c. brown sugar
4 tsp. cinnamon
1 tsp. salt
⅓ c. butter, softened
1 package white or yellow cake mix
1½ to 2 c. fresh or frozen huckleberries (or
    other berries of your choice)

Generously grease and flour a 9-by-13-inch pan.

Mix together the nuts and corn flakes. Add brown sugar, cinnamon, salt and butter and mix thoroughly.

Mix cake mix as directed on package. Put 1½ c. of the crumb mixture on the bottom of prepared pan. Spread batter next, then berries. Top with remaining crumb mixture. Swirl with knife in marble fashion.

Bake at 350 degrees for 35 or 45 minutes, or when touched lightly with finger, the cake gives slightly. This cake is best left in the pan for serving.

Janet Spriet
Baker City, Oregon • Oregon Trail Electric Cooperative

Crazy Chocolate Cake

3 c. flour
2 c. sugar
1 tsp. salt
2 tsp. baking soda
2 oz. unsweetened chocolate, melted
2 Tbsp. white vinegar
¾ c. oil
2 tsp. vanilla
2 c. water

Combine all ingredients in a large bowl. Mix well.

Pour into an ungreased oblong cake pan. Bake for 30 to 40 minutes, or until done. After it is cool, use Cool Whip or a frosting of your choice for the topping.

Mary LaSalle
North Pole, Alaska • Golden Valley Electric Association

Date Nut Salad Cake

½ lb. dates, cut into small pieces
1 c. boiling water
2 tsp. baking soda
1 c. sugar
1 c. salad dressing
2 c. flour
1 tsp. vanilla
1 c. nuts, chopped and floured
Icing:
½ c. brown sugar
¼ c. top milk
2 Tbsp. butter
2 c. powdered sugar
1 tsp. vanilla

Add baking soda to dates. Pour boiling water over this. Stir and let set until cool.

Add sugar, salad dressing, flour, vanilla and nuts. Mix all together and beat thoroughly. Flour the pan. Bake a loaf pan for 55 minutes or two cake pans for 35 minutes at 350 degrees.

To make icing, cook sugar, cream and butter to boiling. Stir in powdered sugar and beat until creamy.

Betty Jane Phillips
West Richland, Washington

Delicious Fruit Cake

3 eggs
¾ c. flour
¾ c. sugar
½ tsp. salt
1 tsp. vanilla
1 jar maraschino cherries, drained
1 lb. pitted dates
2 lbs. walnuts

In a mixing bowl, beat eggs until foamy. Add sugar, flour, salt and vanilla. Stir well and then add the nuts and cherries. Stir until coated.

Pour into two greased 9-by-5-by-3-inch pans. I put wax paper in the bottom of the pans and remove it when baked.

Bake at 350 degrees for 1 hour and 20 minutes.

I have made this for many years and everyone says, "It's the best!" I received this recipe from a relative that has long been gone.

Adelia Olson
Norfolk, Nebraska • Elkhorn Rural Public Power

Devil's Dump Cake

1½ c. flour
1 c. sugar
½ c. ground chocolate
1 tsp. baking soda
½ tsp. salt
1 egg
1 c. buttermilk
½ c. oil
1 tsp. vanilla

Mix all together. Bake at 350 degrees for 30 minutes, or until toothpick comes out clean.

Frost or dust top of cake with powdered sugar.

Kay Antunez de Mayolo
Eagleville, California • Surprise Valley Electrification

Farmer's Cake

2 c. flour
2 c. sugar
2 tsp. cinnamon
2 tsp. baking soda
1 tsp. salt
1½ c. oil
3 eggs
2 tsp. vanilla
2 c. carrots, shredded
16-oz. can crushed pineapple, drained
1 c. chopped nuts
Icing:
2 sticks (1 c.) butter
6 oz. cream cheese
¾ c. powdered sugar

To make cake, combine all ingredients and mix by hand or use mixer on low until well blended. Pour into a buttered and floured 9-by-13-inch pan. Bake at 350 degrees for 50 to 60 minutes.

To make icing, cream butter, cream cheese and powdered sugar with blender until slightly fluffy. Spread icing on cooled cake.

Debi Rossman

Filled Chocolate Cupcakes

Chocolate cake mix
Filling:
8 oz. cream cheese, softened to room temperature
1 egg
⅓ c. sugar
1 tsp. vanilla
1 c. chocolate chips
Frosting:
1½ squares unsweetened chocolate
3 Tbsp. butter
2¼ c. powdered sugar
1½ tsp. vanilla
3 Tbsp. hot water

Prepare cake mix for cupcakes. Pour batter into paper cups in muffin pans.

Beat together cream cheese, egg, sugar and vanilla. Stir in chocolate chips.

Drop the mixture into slight indentation in batter (use spoon to make a small "well").

Bake full time according to directions and a little longer to prevent them from becoming soggy. Cool slowly.

To make frosting, melt chocolate and butter. Add powdered sugar, vanilla and hot water. Stir together quickly and spread on cupcakes while frosting is hot. It will set up.

Having been a home economics major at San Jose State University, I have many wonderful recipes in my collection.

Shirley Hambey
Graeagle, California • Plumas-Sierra Rural Electric Cooperative

Fresh Apple Cake

4 c. apples, diced
2 c. sugar
½ c. salad oil
2 eggs
1 c. nuts
1 tsp. vanilla
2 c. flour
1 tsp. salt
1 tsp. baking soda
2 tsp. cinnamon

Mix together apples, sugar, salad oil, eggs, nuts and vanilla. Add the dry ingredients and mix by hand with a spoon (turn over).

Bake at 350 degrees for 45 minutes to 1 hour. It is done when inserted knife comes out clean.

Brenda Burdick
Spring Creek, Nevada • Wells Rural Electric

Incredible Coconut Cake

5 eggs, separated
2 c. sugar
½ c. butter, softened
½ c. canola oil
1 tsp. coconut extract
¼ tsp. almond extract
½ tsp. vanilla extract
2¼ c. cake flour
1 tsp. baking powder
½ tsp. baking soda
¼ tsp. salt
1 c. buttermilk
2 c. flaked coconut, chopped
¼ tsp. cream of tartar

Frosting:

2 packages (one 8 oz., one 3 oz.) cream cheese, softened
⅔ c. butter, softened
4⅓ c. confectioners' sugar
1¼ tsp. coconut extract
2 c. flaked coconut, toasted

Place egg whites in large bowl. Let stand at room temperature for 30 minutes. In another large bowl, beat the sugar, butter and oil until light and fluffy. Add yolks, one at a time, beating well after each addition. Beat in extracts.

Combine the flour, baking powder, baking soda and salt. Add to creamed mixture alternately with buttermilk, beating well after each addition. Stir in coconut.

Add cream of tartar to egg whites; beat until stiff peaks form. Gently fold into batter.

Transfer to three greased and floured 9-inch round baking pans. Bake at 325 degrees for 25 to 30 minutes, or until toothpick inserted near center comes out clean. Cool for 10 minutes before removing from pans to wire racks to cool completely.

For frosting, beat cream cheese and butter in a small bowl until fluffy. Add confectioners' sugar and extract; beat until smooth.

Place one cake layer on a serving plate. Spread with ½ c. frosting and sprinkle with ⅓ c. coconut. Repeat. Top with remaining cake layer. Spread remaining frosting over the top and sides of cake. Sprinkle with remaining coconut.

Refrigerate for two hours before cutting. Store in the refrigerator.

This is my all-time favorite cake. And my friends love it, too. You could say I have a cult following regarding this cake.

Charlotte Beaudry
Trout Creek, Montana

Lemon-Glazed Cheesecake

Crust:

2 c. gingersnap cookies, finely crushed
   (or graham cracker crumbs)
6 Tbsp. melted butter
2 Tbsp. sugar

Filling:

3 8-oz. packages cream cheese (1½ lb.)
¾ c. sugar
3 eggs
¼ c. lemon juice
2 tsp. lemon rind, grated
2 tsp. vanilla

Topping:

2 c. sour cream
3 Tbsp. sugar
1 tsp. vanilla
Ground cinnamon, to taste

Garnish (optional):

Lemon strip
Strawberry
Mint leaves

Preheat oven to 350 degrees. Combine crust ingredients thoroughly. Press crust evenly onto bottom and sides of buttered 9-by-3-inch springform pan. Bake 5 minutes. Cool.

Beat cream cheese until soft. Add sugar, blending thoroughly. Add eggs, one at a time, beating well after each addition. Mix in lemon juice, rind and vanilla. Blend well. Turn into springform pan. Bake for 35 minutes.

While cake is baking, blend sour cream, sugar and vanilla. Remove cake from oven. Sprinkle with ground cinnamon. Gently spread sour cream mixture over top. Return to oven and bake for 12 minutes. Cool on a rack for 30 minutes.

Spread with lemon glaze (see below). Chill several hours or, preferably, overnight, before removing sides of pan. Garnish with lemon strip, strawberry and mint leaves.

Lemon glaze:

½ c. sugar
1½ Tbsp. cornstarch
¼ tsp. salt
¾ c. water
⅓ c. lemon juice
1 egg yolk
1 Tbsp. butter
1 tsp. grated lemon rind
2 to 3 drops yellow food coloring (optional)

In a heavy 1-quart saucepan, mix sugar, cornstarch and salt. Combine water, lemon juice and egg yolk and add to sugar mixture. Cook over low heat, stirring constantly, until the mixture comes to a slow boil and is thickened.

Add butter and lemon rind. At this point, you can also add yellow food coloring, if desired. Allow to cool slightly, but spread on cheesecake before glaze sets.

Mary Ann Brolin
Blairsden, California • Plumas-Sierra Rural Electric Cooperative

Mexican Fruit Cake

2 c. flour
2 c. sugar or sugar substitute
20-oz. can crushed pineapple, including juice
2 eggs
2 tsp. baking soda
1 c. nuts, chopped
Icing:
8 oz. cream cheese, softened
1 stick margarine, softened
2 c. powdered sugar
1 tsp. vanilla

Heat oven to 350 degrees. Mix together flour, sugar, pineapple, eggs, baking soda and nuts by hand. Put into ungreased 8-by-12-inch pan. Do not use a glass pan.

Bake for 35 to 40 minutes.

To make icing, beat ingredients with a hand mixer. Icing will be thin. Make sure cake is completely cooled. Keep refrigerated.

Aileen Benson
Sutherlin, Oregon

Mom's Apple Cake

4 or 5 apples, peeled, cored and diced
2 eggs, beaten slightly
1 tsp. vanilla
1 c. packed brown sugar
3½ c. flour
2 tsp. baking soda
1 c. oil
½ c. milk
1 c. granulated sugar
1 c. walnuts

Cream the oil, eggs, milk, vanilla and both sugars. Sift the dry ingredients and mix with the creamed mixture. Add the apples and walnuts. Bake in a greased 9-by-13-inch pan or a Bundt pan. Bake at 325 degrees for one hour, or until a knife inserted comes out clean.

Sue Troxell
Roy, Washington • Valley Electric Association

Old-Fashioned Raisin Cake

3 c. raisins
2 c. sugar
2 tsp. cinnamon
Dash of nutmeg
1⅓ c. Crisco
4 c. water
⅔ tsp. salt
2 tsp. baking soda
2 tsp. baking powder
4 c. flour

Cook and boil raisins, sugar, cinnamon, nutmeg, Crisco, water and salt in a large pot for about 3 minutes. Cool, then add baking soda, baking powder and flour.

Mix together and bake in a 9-by-13-inch inch pan that has been floured and greased, or use cooking spray. Bake in a 350-degree oven for 45 minutes. Test for doneness with a toothpick in the middle of the cake; the toothpick should come out clean.

Nancy Storlie
Fairbanks, Alaska • Golden Valley Electric Association

Orange Dream Delicacy

2 large egg yolks, beaten
1 c. sugar
2 Tbsp. all-purpose flour
1 pinch kosher salt
1 c. whole milk
1 orange, zest and juice
2 tsp. vanilla extract
2 Tbsp. unsalted butter, melted
2 large egg whites, beaten to stiff peaks
Preheat oven to 350 degrees.

In a large bowl, mix together egg yolks and sugar. Sift in the flour and salt; mix together. Add the milk, orange zest and juice, vanilla and melted butter. Fold in egg whites just until incorporated. Pour into a greased baking dish.

Put baking dish in a larger baking dish. Pour hot water one-third of the way full, and bake for 30 to 35 minutes.

Remove the cake and cool prior to serving.

David Wilson
La Grange, Illinois • Commonwealth Edison

Pineapple/Fruit/Walnut Cake

2 sticks butter
1 c. brown sugar
2 tsp. baking soda
2 c. flour
15-oz. can fruit cocktail, drained
2 eggs
8-oz. can crushed pineapple, in its own juice, undrained
Walnuts, chopped

Mix everything except nuts with an electric mixer. Pour into a greased and floured 9-by-13-inch pan. Sprinkle nuts on batter. Bake at 325 degrees for 55 minutes.

Topping:

1 stick butter
1 tsp. vanilla
½ c. sugar
1 c. coconut
5.3 oz. whipping cream

Mix all ingredients and bring to boil slowly, stirring to prevent burning, until thick. Pour over cake.

Barbara L. Rexford
Bonners Ferry, Idaho · Northern Lights

Pumpkin Roll

3 eggs
1 c. sugar
⅔ c. cooked pumpkin
1 c. chopped pecans
¾ c. all-purpose flour
1 tsp. baking powder
½ tsp. salt
1 tsp. cinnamon
½ tsp. allspice
¼ tsp. nutmeg
1 tsp. lemon juice

Beat eggs for 5 minutes at high speed. Gradually add sugar, then pumpkin mixed with lemon juice. Sift flour and spices together. Add to previous mixture. Spread in a greased and floured (or wax-paper lined) 15-by-10-inch pan. Top with chopped nuts, pressing them gently into the batter.

Bake at 350 degrees for 15 minutes. Be careful not to over bake; bake until set well.

Remove pan from oven and loosen edges well. Turn into a towel that has been sprinkled generously with powdered sugar. Roll towel and cake up together jelly-roll style and let cool. While cake is cooling, make the filling.

Filling:

1 c. powdered sugar
8 oz. cream cheese
6 Tbsp. butter
1 tsp. vanilla

Combine ingredients and beat until smooth. Spread filling over cooled cake. Re-roll and wrap in foil. Keep refrigerated.

Amy M. Kyser
Southport, Florida · Gulf Coast Electric Cooperative

Snowman Cake Pops

1 c. white sugar
½ c. butter
2 eggs
2 tsp. vanilla extract
1½ c. all-purpose flour
1¾ tsp. baking powder
½ c. milk
1 can of cream cheese frosting
1 bag of Hershey's bell-shaped candy
White sprinkles
Snowflake sprinkles
Orange sprinkles
Cake pop sticks
White almond bark
Brown almond bark
Styrofoam block

Preheat oven to 350 degrees. Spray a Bundt pan with cooking spray.

In a mixing bowl, cream together sugar and butter. Beat in eggs one at a time, then add vanilla. Sift together flour and baking powder. Slowly add in dry ingredients until thoroughly mixed. Stir in the milk until the batter is smooth.

Pour the cake batter into the prepared Bundt pan. Bake for 45 minutes, or until a toothpick comes out clean. Allow the cake to cool completely.

Crumble the cake into a large mixing bowl. Add small amounts of cream cheese frosting until a sticky texture is formed (for a whole cake you will use around half a can). Using a scoop or spoon, take some of the cake mixture and roll into a ball. After all the balls have been formed, place them on a baking sheet lined with wax paper in the freezer for 5 to 10 minutes.

Melt white almond bark according to package instructions. Dip the tip of a cake pop stick into the melted bark and insert the stick into the bottom of the formed cake balls (about half way). Allow to dry.

Submerge the entire pop into the melted white bark and tap off the excess. Before the bark can dry place the Hershey's bell "hat" on top of the ball (snowman's head) and apply white sprinkles to the entire pop. Place on a Styrofoam block to dry.

Dip a cake pop stick into brown melted bark, dot on eyes and mouth.

Place a dot of the brown bark on the hat and add snowflake sprinkle. Dip a cake pop stick into the white melted bark and dab onto the nose area of the snowman's face. Apply orange sprinkle for the nose.

Brittney Syrie
Union, Oregon

Sour Cream Coffee Cake

1 c. butter or oleo
1¼ c. sugar
2 eggs, beaten
1 c. sour cream
1 tsp. vanilla
2 c. flour, sifted
1 tsp. baking powder
½ tsp. baking soda
3 Tbsp. powdered sugar
Topping:
1 c. nuts, finely chopped
2 Tbsp. sugar
½ tsp. cinnamon

Cream butter and sugar. Add beaten eggs, sour cream and vanilla. Beat well. Gradually add sifted flour, baking powder and soda. When mixture gets too thick to beat, stir until well mixed.

Place half of the mixture in a 9-inch tube pan and sprinkle with half of the topping mixture. Place remaining dough mixture on top and sprinkle with the rest of the topping mixture.

Bake for one hour at 350 degrees, or until an inserted knife comes out clean.

Sprinkle powdered sugar on top while still hot. Cool 15 to 20 minutes before cutting.

Rosemary Hart
Casa Grande, Arizona • Electrical District No. 2

Upside Down Cake

⅓ c. butter
1 c. brown sugar
1 large can pineapple chunks (or any fresh or
    canned fruit), well drained; reserve juice
2 eggs
1 c. sugar
1 tsp. baking powder
½ tsp. baking soda
1 c. flour
⅓ c. orange juice (optional)

In an iron skillet, melt butter and brown sugar. Add the pineapple chunks. Set iron skillet aside.

In your mixer, beat eggs until frothy. Add sugar and beat until thick. Add baking powder, baking soda and flour. Keep beating, and add ⅓ c. juice from the pineapple, or ⅓ c. orange juice if you use fresh fruit.

Pour the batter over the fruit and brown sugar in the skillet. Bake at 325 degrees for 55 minutes, or until a toothpick comes out clean.

Take the skillet from the oven and run a knife around the outside edge. Put a plate on top and invert the skillet onto the plate. The cake is ready to eat with whip cream, ice cream or just plain and warm from the oven.

Note: You can double this and make in a 9-by-13-inch glass or metal pan; you just have to melt the butter in the microwave. Also, if you don't have an iron skillet, a 9-by-9 inch pan will work.

This recipe has been in our family for over 70 years, passed down from my mom to me and now being made by my daughters.

Sally Cutting
Monroe, Oregon • Consumers Power

Yummy Raw Apple Cake

2 eggs, slightly beaten
1½ c. sugar
¾ c. canola oil
2 tsp. vanilla
¼ c. water
2 c. flour
2 tsp. baking soda
½ tsp. salt
½ tsp. cinnamon
6 c. apples, unpeeled and cut in small pieces
½ c. raisins
½ c. shredded coconut
Topping:
8 oz. cream cheese
4 c. confectioners' sugar
1 tsp. vanilla
Walnuts, chopped (optional)

Mix eggs, sugar, oil, vanilla and water together.

In a separate bowl, mix together flour, baking soda, salt and cinnamon. Add dry mixture to wet mixture. Blend well.

Mix in apple pieces, raisins and coconut.

Pour batter into a greased 9-by-13-inch pan. Bake at 350

degrees for 35 to 40 minutes.

To make the topping, mix together cream cheese, confectioners' sugar and vanilla. Spread on cooled cake. Sprinkle with walnuts.

Rosalva Lemmon
Prosser, Washington • Benton Rural Electric Association

Desserts: Cobbler

Jim's Blackberry Cobbler

4 c. blackberries, thawed if frozen
2 Tbsp. cornstarch
¾ c. all-purpose flour
¾ tsp. baking powder
⅓ c. sugar
¼ tsp. salt
¼ tsp. cinnamon
¼ tsp. ground cloves
¼ tsp. nutmeg
6 Tbsp. butter or margarine
1 tsp. vanilla
⅓ c. milk
⅓ c. water
¾ c. sugar

Preheat oven to 350 degrees. Mix cornstarch and berries thoroughly in a two-quart baking dish.

In a small bowl, combine ⅓ c. sugar, baking powder, salt, flour and spices.

In a separate bowl, combine butter, vanilla and milk, then add to dry mixture. Mix until free of lumps.

Spoon batter over top of berries. Mix ⅓ c. water with ¾ c. sugar. Pour on top of batter.

Bake for 45 minutes, or until top is golden brown. Serve warm or let it cool. Top with extra creamy Cool Whip or vanilla ice cream.

I have made this cobbler for several years. I pick and freeze a lot of blackberries and I make a big cobbler for our Christmas dinner. It does not last long!

Jim Proffitt
The Dalles, Oregon • Northern Wasco PUD

Mom's Cherry Cinnamon Roll Cobbler

½ c. sugar
2 to 4 Tbsp. red cinnamon candies
2 Tbsp. cornstarch
½ c. water
1 can sour pie cherries or 1 lb. frozen cherries; reserve juice

Combine sugar, cinnamon candies, cornstarch, water and cherry juice in a saucepan. Cook over medium heat, stirring occasionally, until thickened. Stir in cherries. Pour into an 8-by-8-inch baking dish.

Cinnamon rounds:

1½ c. sifted plain flour
2 tsp. baking powder
½ tsp. salt
6 Tbsp. brown sugar, divided
⅓ c. pecans, finely chopped
¼ c. shortening
1 egg, slightly beaten
2 Tbsp. milk
1 Tbsp. butter, soft
¼ tsp. cinnamon

Sift flour with baking powder and salt into a mixing bowl. Add 3 Tbsp. brown sugar and pecans. Cut in shortening until particles are fine. Combine egg and milk. Add to flour mixture and mix until all dry particles are moistened, adding a few drops more of milk, if necessary.

Roll out on floured surface to a 14-by-12-inch rectangle. Brush with butter. Combine 3 Tbsp. brown sugar and cinnamon; sprinkle over dough. Roll up, starting with the 12-inch side. Cut into ¾-inch slices. Place on cherry filling. Bake at 400 degrees for 25 to 30 minutes.

You also can substitute peaches for the cherries. Use canned peaches or six medium peeled peaches. Omit cinnamon candies, and proceed with the same filling process.

My mom, Hazel Brown, would make this often for our family. Everyone who has tried this recipe has never been disappointed. It gives a different, unique and delicious twist to cobbler.

Elizabeth Suggs
Okeechobee, Florida • Glades Electric Cooperative

Southern-Style Blackberry Cobbler

1½ c. fresh-picked blackberries
2 c. sugar, divided
1 c. flour
1 c. buttermilk
1 tsp. baking powder
¼ c. water

Preheat oven to 350 degrees. Wash and drain berries. Place berries in saucepan along with water and 1 c. sugar. Stir together and bring to a boil. Simmer for 10 to 15 minutes while continuing to stir.

Mix dry ingredients together in a baking dish, then fold buttermilk into mixture. Poke holes through batter before adding cooked berries, pouring in slowly and allowing the sauce to seep through the batter.

Bake at 350 degrees for 30 to 45 minutes, until golden brown on top.

Note: Other berries/fruits such as peaches or apples may be substituted.

Rhonda Turner
Goldendale, Washington • Klickitat County PUD

Summery Mango Cobbler

3 c. mangoes, peeled and sliced
1 c. white sugar, divided
½ c. water
9 Tbsp. butter, divided
1¼ c. flour, divided
1 tsp. baking powder
¼ tsp. salt
½ c. milk or cream
2 tsp. cinnamon
½ c. quick-cooking oats
½ c. brown sugar

Preheat oven to 350 degrees. Combine mangoes, ½ c. of the white sugar and the water in a heavy saucepan on the stove. Bring to a boil, then simmer for 10 minutes, or until syrup has thickened. Remove from heat.

Melt 4 Tbsp. butter in a 3-quart glass baking dish. In a medium bowl, mix the remaining ½ c. white sugar, ¾ c. flour, baking powder, salt and milk until just combined. Pour the mixture slowly over the melted butter in the baking dish. Sprinkle with cinnamon.

Using a slotted spoon, transfer mangoes from saucepan onto the batter in the baking dish. Spoon mango syrup over the top, reserving ½ c. of the syrup for later use.

Mix the remaining ½ c. flour with the oats and brown sugar in a medium bowl. Cut in remaining 5 Tbsp. butter and mix with fingers until combined. Use fingers to drop topping evenly over cobbler.

Bake at 350 degrees for 30 to 35 minutes, until cobbler is golden brown.

Ladle into bowls while still warm and top each serving with some of the reserved mango syrup, and vanilla ice cream, if desired.

Melissa Elbert
Palmetto, Florida • Peace River Electric Cooperative

Desserts: Cookies

Chocolate Caramel Brownie Cookies

½ c. sugar
½ c. brown sugar
½ c. mayonnaise
2 Tbsp. oleo
2 c. flour
¼ c. to ½ c. semisweet baking cocoa
½ tsp. baking soda
½ tsp. salt
Chocolate syrup
Caramel syrup

In a small bowl, combine flour, cocoa, baking soda and salt. Set aside.

In a larger bowl, combine sugar, brown sugar, mayonnaise and oleo. Slowly add flour mixture, adding enough flour so batter feels tacky to touch. It will be slightly thick.

In an 8-by-8-inch glass baking dish, bake on lower rack at 325 degrees for 10 minutes.

Remove from oven and drizzle with chocolate and caramel syrups.

Return to oven and bake an additional 10 minutes at 350 degrees. Cool for 10 minutes.

Sydney R. Bowe
Hermiston, Oregon • Umatilla Electric Cooperative

Chocolate Oatmeal Cookies

½ c. sugar
½ c. light brown sugar
½ c. mayonnaise
1 Tbsp. oil
3 Tbsp. milk
2 c. flour
¼ to ½ c. semisweet baking cocoa
½ tsp. baking soda

½ tsp. salt

Topping:

½ c. brown sugar

¼ c. semisweet baking cocoa

In a small bowl, combine flour, cocoa, baking soda and salt. Set aside.

In a larger bowl, combine sugar, brown sugar, mayonnaise, oil and milk. Slowly add flour mixture, adding enough flour so batter feels tacky to touch, and slightly thick.

In an 8-by-8-inch glass baking dish, bake on lower rack at 325 degrees for 10 minutes.

Remove from oven and add topping mixure. Return to oven and bake at 350 degrees for an additional 10 minutes. Cool for 10 minutes.

Sydney R. Bowe
Hermiston, Oregon • Umatilla Electric Cooperative

Gluten-Free Chocolate Chip Cookies

1½ cubes butter

½ c. sugar

1 tsp. vanilla

2 eggs

½ c. corn flour

½ c. buckwheat flour

½ c. rice flour

¼ c. coconut flour

½ c. flax meal

1 tsp. baking soda

1½ c. chocolate or carob chips

1½ c. walnuts, chopped

With electric mixer, cream together butter and sugars (I use my mixer with the dough hook to mix all the ingredients). Then add vanilla and eggs.

In a separate bowl, combine the soda, flours and flax meal. Gradually add flour mixture to mixing bowl; mix well. Add nuts and chocolate chips and mix well. Drop by rounded spoonfuls on a cookie sheet and bake for 8 to 10 minutes at 375 degrees.

Roxanne Clough
Kamiah, Idaho • Idaho County Light and Power

Ice Box Cookies (aka Refrigerator Cookies)

2 c. brown sugar

1 c. Crisco

2 eggs

1 tsp. baking soda

2 to 3 tsp. vanilla

3 c. flour

1 c. nuts, chopped

Cream sugar and shortening. Add eggs and vanilla and mix well. Add dry ingredients and nuts and mix well. Split into rolls or squares and wrap in wax paper or plastic wrap. Refrigerate for up to a week or freeze for up to a month.

Slice and bake at 350 degrees for 5 to 8 minutes, depending on if you like them softer or crunchier and how thick you slice them.

The flavor will change depending on the kind of nuts you use. You can use butter or flavored Crisco or plain Crisco. You also can use white sugar in place of the brown.

These were our family traditional Christmas cookies. There were six of us kids and we were all playing basketball. My mom always made tons and then would slice and bake a batch for one of us to take on the bus trips when we went to tournaments over the Christmas holidays. They continue to be a favorite part of the Christmas season for all of us.

Tracy Blais
Delta Junction, Alaska • Golden Valley Electric Association

Joy's No-Bake Cookies

2 c. sugar

½ c. butter

½ c. milk

4 tsp. cocoa

½ c. peanut butter

1 tsp. vanilla

3 c. oatmeal

Boil sugar, butter, milk and cocoa for 2 minutes. Cool mixture and add peanut butter and vanilla. Stir in oatmeal. Drop by spoonfuls on waxed paper. Cool in freezer or refrigerator.

Charmaree Cook
North Pole, Alaska • Golden Valley Electric Association

Lacey Chocolate Macaroons

3 egg whites, at room temperature
½ tsp. vanilla
1½ c. powdered sugar
⅓ c. cocoa powder
¾ c. walnuts, chopped
¾ to 1 c. unsweetened shredded coconut

Grease a baking sheet well. Preheat oven to 350 degrees.

Beat the egg whites until they begin to foam, slowly increasing the speed until the foam forms stiff, glossy peaks. This will take several minutes. Add the vanilla extract.

With a spatula, fold in the powdered sugar, cocoa, walnuts and coconut until just combined. It is important to handle the batter as little as possible.

Spoon the batter onto the pan in rounded mounds. It should stand as a mound ¾-inch high on the pan. If it's too thick, add more coconut.

Bake for 15 to 18 minutes, until light brown. The longer they cook, the larger and thinner they will be.

Immediately remove the cookies with a thin metal spatula. Be careful to loosen the edge of the cookie by sawing the spatula back and forth. Cool the cookies on a wire rack.

Amy Hackbarth
Bend, Oregon • Central Electric Cooperative

Molasses Cookies

1 c. butter
2 c. brown sugar
2 eggs
½ c. molasses
¼ tsp. salt
4 tsp. cinnamon
4 tsp. ginger
4 tsp. baking soda
4 c. flour
Granulated sugar

Mix butter, sugar and eggs. Stir in molasses, salt, baking soda and spices until mixed well. Add flour.

Form into small balls and roll in granulated sugar. Bake at 350 degrees for 8 to 10 minutes.

Stephanie Rider
Monroe, Washington

Monster Cookies

3 eggs
1½ c. packed brown sugar
1 c. white sugar
1 tsp. vanilla
1 tsp. corn syrup
2 tsp. baking soda
½ c. butter, softened
1½ c. crunchy peanut butter
4½ c. rolled quick oats
1 c. M&M's
1 c. chocolate chips

Mix everything except oats, M&M's, and chips. Add oats and mix well. Add M&M's and chocolate chips.

Form large balls and press into thick rounds on a baking stone or cookie sheet. Bake at 350 degrees for 17 minutes, or until cookies are golden brown. Do not overcook for soft cookies.

Chelsea Scilzo
Dillingham, Alaska • Nushagak Cooperative

Oatmeal Cookies

1½ c. sugar
1 tsp. baking powder
3½ c. whole-wheat pastry flour
1 c. milk or 1½ c. applesauce
4½ c. regular oats
4 eggs
2 c. raisins
1 c. oil
2 c. chopped walnuts
1 c. chocolate chips (optional)
2 tsp. baking soda
2 tsp. salt
2 tsp. vanilla
2 tsp. cinnamon

Combine dry ingredients. Stir in remaining ingredients. Drop by big spoonfuls, about the size of an egg, onto a greased cookie sheet. Bake at 350 degrees for about 15 minutes, or until tested done.

These hearty, healthy cookies have been a family favorite for a long time. My son eats them for a fast, easy breakfast.

Michelle Stace
Terrebonne, Oregon • Central Electric Cooperative

Oatmeal Macaroons

½ c. shortening
1 c. sugar
1 Tbsp. molasses
1 tsp. vanilla
1 egg
1 c. flour
¼ tsp. salt
1 tsp. cinnamon
¾ tsp. baking soda
1 c. oats
½ c. raisins
½ c. dates, chopped
½ c. nuts, chopped
Mix everything together. Bake at 350 degrees for 10 to 15 minutes.

Jo Tarver
Corvallis, Oregon • Consumers Power

Orange Cookie Balls

½ c. butter
1 c. sugar
⅓ c. frozen orange juice, undiluted
½ c. coconut
½ c. walnuts, finely chopped
7-oz. package vanilla wafers, crushed (2½ c.)
Cream together butter, sugar and frozen orange juice. Add coconut, walnuts and vanilla wafers.

Mix all ingredients and chill before forming into balls. Roll balls in sifted powdered sugar. Refrigerate. They are better after two to three days.

Shirley Hambey
Graeagle, California • Plumas-Sierra Rural Electric Cooperative

Sweet Dreams

1 box white cake mix
1 stick butter, softened
½ c. applesauce
2 eggs
½ c. powdered sugar
Cream eggs, butter and applesauce together and add to the cake mix. Stir with spoon until lumps are gone.

Drop by teaspoon-sized dough into powdered sugar and cover completely.

Bake at 350 degrees on a greased cookie sheet for approximately 8 minutes.

Teena Patterson
Irrigon, Oregon • Umatilla Electric Cooperative

Desserts: Pies

Brown Paper Bag Apple Pie

9-inch pie crust, unbaked
6 to 8 apples, peeled and cut up
1 c. sugar, divided
½ c. and 2 Tbsp. flour
½ stick margarine
½ tsp. cinnamon
¼ tsp. nutmeg
Mix ½ c. sugar with 2 Tbsp. flour. Mix with apples and pour into pie crust.

Mix together remaining sugar, ½ c. flour, margarine, cinnamon and nutmeg until crumbly; sprinkle over apples.

Place pie in a brown paper bag and fold the end of the bag over, fastening it with a paper clip. Bake for 1 hour at 400 degrees.

Hazel Wilson
Molino, Florida • Escambia River Electric Cooperative

Carrot Pie

3 cans sliced carrots, drained
1 c. light brown sugar
1 tsp. allspice
½ tsp. cinnamon
2 large eggs
1 tsp. vanilla
9-inch pie shell
Put carrots in food processor and blend well. Add remaining ingredients and blend with carrots.

Pour into unbaked pie shell. Bake at 325 degrees for 55 minutes, or until knife inserted in the center comes out clean.

Remove from oven and cool completely. Add favorite whipped topping and enjoy.

This has become my kids' all-time favorite pie.

Daisy K. Richardson
Zolfo Springs, Florida • Peace River Electric Cooperative

Cherry-O Cream Pie

8 oz. cream cheese, softened
14-oz. can sweetened condensed milk
½ c. lemon juice
1 tsp. vanilla
1 lb., 5 oz. cherry pie filling, chilled
9-inch premade graham cracker crust

Using a mixer at medium speed, beat the cream cheese until light and fluffy, then add the condensed milk. Blend thoroughly until smooth. Stir in lemon juice and vanilla. Turn into the crust.

Cover and chill for two to three hours. Top with chilled cherry filling before serving.

This is one of our family's favorites and everyone else who's had it, too.

Lisa Marie Hellmer
Pahrump, Nevada • Valley Electric Association

Chess Pie Tartlets

3 c. flour
1 tsp. salt
2½ c. and 1 Tbsp. sugar
½ c. shortening
6 Tbsp. cold water
1 Tbsp. white vinegar
1 small egg
1½ c. butter
4 eggs
3 egg whites
2½ tsp. vanilla
2¾ c. raisins
2¼ c. walnuts, chopped

Sift together flour, salt and 1 Tbsp. sugar. Cut in shortening. Add water, white vinegar and small egg; mix.

Roll into a ball shape using a small amount of flour until smooth. Divide into 24 small balls, roll into small circles and place in muffin pans.

Cream butter, 2½ c. sugar, 4 eggs and egg whites. Add vanilla, raisins and walnuts.

Put raisin and walnut mixture into the pastry shells in the muffin pans.

Bake at 375 degrees for 10 minutes, then bake at 350 degrees for an additional 20 minutes.

Let tarts cool in the muffin tins for 15 minutes, then remove them.

Jean Dillard
Bend, Oregon • Midstate Electric

Chris' Yummy Apple Pie

2 prepared pie crusts for a 9-inch pie pan
½ c. unsalted butter
3 Tbsp. all-purpose flour
½ c. white sugar
½ c. packed brown sugar
8 Granny Smith apples, peeled, cored and sliced (I use
   a variety of apples to make about 6 to 7 cups)
1 Tbsp. vanilla

Preheat oven to 425 degrees. Melt the butter in a saucepan, then stir in the flour to form a paste. Add the water, vanilla and both sugars, and bring the mixture to a boil. Reduce the temperature and let simmer.

Place the bottom crust in the pan and fill with the sliced apples until it is mounded slightly. Cover with a lattice work crust. Gently pour the sugar/butter mixture over the crust. Pour slowly so that it does not run off.

Bake 15 minutes in preheated oven. Reduce the temperature to 350 degrees and continue baking for 35 to 45 minutes, until the apples are soft.

Sue Troxell
Roy, Washington • Valley Electric Association

Crumbly Apple Pie

Crust:
1 c. flour
½ tsp. salt
⅓ c. butter
¼ c. ice water

Topping:
¾ c. packed brown sugar
¾ c. flour
½ tsp. ground nutmeg
⅓ c. chilled butter, cut into small pieces

Filling:
7 medium (6 c.) Granny Smith, Golden Delicious or almost
   any sweet-tart apple, peeled, cored and sliced thinly
½ c. granulated sugar
1 tsp. ground cinnamon
¼ tsp. ground nutmeg
¼ tsp. salt
3 Tbsp. flour

I always prepare the crust and topping before I prepare the filling. If you prepare the filling first, the salt tends to draw the liquid out of the apple slices before you get the crust and topping done.

To prepare crust: In a medium bowl, mix together flour and

salt. Using a pastry blender or two knives, cut butter into flour mixture until coarse crumbs form.

Add water, 1 Tbsp. at a time, stirring lightly with a spoon until dough forms.

Shape into a disk, wrap in plastic wrap and chill for 30 minutes. On a floured surface, using a floured rolling pin, roll dough into a 12-inch circle. Fit into a 9-inch pie pan. Shape excess dough into a decorative edge.

To prepare topping: In a small bowl, mix together brown sugar, flour and nutmeg. Using a pastry blender or two knives, cut butter into brown sugar mixture until coarse crumbs form.

To prepare filling: Mix together all ingredients. Spoon into crust. Sprinkle apples evenly with topping.

Place oven rack in lowest position; preheat oven to 400 degrees. Bake pie until topping is lightly browned and filling is bubbly, about 35 minutes. If pie is over-browning, cover loosely with aluminum foil. Transfer to a wire rack to cool.

Charles Rossman

Fresh Strawberry Pie

1 qt. strawberries
1 pie crust
1 box strawberry Jell-O
2 Tbsp. cornstarch
1½ c. water
Splenda

Put water and cornstarch in a small saucepan. Stir constantly to boil. Add Jell-O and boil for two minutes. Take off heat and set in larger pan with ice to cool.

Place pie crust in oven at 375 degrees and bake for 10 to 12 minutes. Cool crust on table on cold towels.

Wash berries and hull. In cool crust, slice berries and add a little Splenda. Continue to slice berries; top with small amount of Splenda over top.

Take thoroughly cooled Jell-O and spoon on berries to cover. Refrigerate several hours.

Cool Whip or Reddi-Whip are the final touch when serving.

I make especially for my diabetic friends; it's nicer than a dish of Jell-O.

Rose Lausman
Lake Placid, Florida • Glades Electric Cooperative

Kahlua Pie

1½ c. dark chocolate
½ c. whipping cream
8 oz. cream cheese
⅔ c. Kahlua
16 oz. whipped cream
Pie shell, baked

Melt dark chocolate and whipping cream in the microwave. Mix cream cheese in a food processor and slowly add Kahlua.

Add these mixtures together and fold in whipped cream. Pour into pie shell and refrigerate a couple of hours or freeze.

Kathy Jones
Corvallis, Oregon • Consumers Power

Peanut Butter Pie

1 graham cracker crust
1 c. peanut butter
8 oz. cream cheese
1 c. sugar
2 Tbsp. butter, melted
1 c. whipping cream
1 tsp. vanilla
Hot fudge topping

Cream together peanut butter, cream cheese, sugar and melted butter. Set aside.

Whip cream and add vanilla. Combine the two mixtures and pour into the graham cracker crust.

Refrigerate overnight. Half an hour before serving, top the pie with melted hot fudge topping. Chill another 30 minutes.

Carie Mace
Bend, Oregon • Central Electric

Pecan Pie

1 c. light corn syrup
¾ c. sugar
1 cube butter, melted
3 eggs
1 tsp. vanilla
¾ c. pecan pieces
¾ c. pecan halves
9-inch homemade pie crust, unbaked

Mix syrup and sugar. Add melted butter. Mix in eggs and vanilla. Let stand, covered with plastic wrap, for 1 hour. Use a whisk to mix, not an electric mixer.

Place pecan pieces in the unbaked pie shell. Pour in the filling and cover with pecan halves. I like to choose nice, unbroken halves, and place them in a concentric circular pattern. Cover the rim of the crust with foil so it doesn't get too well done.

Bake at 325 degrees for 45 to 50 minutes. Sometimes it takes longer; keep checking until the pie is firm, or until only the very center of the pie moves when you jiggle it.

Place on a rack to cool. Serve with whipped cream or vanilla ice cream.

This pie is always requested by family and friends every Thanksgiving and Christmas. I usually have to make several.

Jan Haugh
Challis, Idaho • Salmon River Electric Cooperative

Pumpkin Pie

4 c. pureed pumpkin
5 c. milk
½ c. flour
3 c. sugar
8 egg yolks
3 tsp. vanilla
½ tsp. salt
1 tsp. cinnamon
½ tsp. cloves
½ tsp. nutmeg
8 egg whites
4 prepared pie crusts

Blend the first 10 ingredients together until smooth. In a separate bowl, beat egg whites until stiff, then fold into pumpkin mixture.

Pour filling into prepared crusts and sprinkle tops with cinnamon.

Bake at 350 degrees for 45 minutes, or until done.

Mrs. Marcus Plank
Alturas, California • Surprise Valley Electrification

Raspberry Pie Crisp

Crust:
2¼ c. flour
¾ tsp. salt
⅔ c. vegetable oil
¼ c. cold water
Filling:
4 c. raspberries, lightly mashed
1¼ c. sugar
3 Tbsp. cornstarch
Topping mix:
½ c. butter, softened
¾ c. flour
⅔ c. brown sugar
1 c. oatmeal
1 tsp. cinnamon

To make the crust: In a 9-by-13-inch baking pan, mix flour, salt, vegetable oil and cold water. Mix well. Press mixture on bottom of pan and an inch up on the sides.

To make the filling: Blend together raspberries, sugar and cornstarch. Cook until thickened and pour over crust mixture.

To make the topping: Blend topping ingredients and sprinkle on top of raspberries. Bake at 375 degrees for 35 minutes.

Serve with whipped cream or ice cream.

Judy Montgomery
Ellensburg, Washington • Kittitas County PUD

Razzed-Up Chocolate Key Lime Pie

Crust:
Prepared chocolate graham cracker crust
Lime curd:
4 Tbsp. unsalted butter
¾ c. sugar
3 eggs
⅓ c. fresh-squeezed key lime juice
1 Tbsp. lime zest
Pie filling:
¾ c. heavy whipping cream
3 Tbsp. powdered sugar
Garnish:
1 c. fresh raspberries, divided
Whipped cream, optional

Prepare the lime curd by creaming butter and sugar until fluffy. Beat in eggs slowly, then add lime juice and zest. The mixture will look curdled, but will become satiny-smooth as it cooks.

Cook over low to medium-low heat, stirring often and

scraping the sides and bottom of pan. Do not allow curd to boil. Cook until it is thick enough your finger can trace a path in the curd as it coats the back of a spoon. Strain the curd through a sieve and cool to room temperature.

In a large bowl, beat whipping cream and powdered sugar until soft peaks form. Blend in cooled lime curd. Place about ¾ c. fresh raspberries evenly over the bottom of the prepared pie crust and spread lime curd mixture on top. Refrigerate for at least 3 hours, or until ready to serve. Garnish with remaining raspberries and whipped cream, if desired.

Melissa Elbert
Palmetto, Florida • Peace River Electric Cooperative

So Easy Chocolate Pie

20 large marshmallows
½ c. milk
1 large Hershey with almonds candy bar
1 pt. whipping cream
Sugar
Crust (regular baked pie crust, graham cracker
   crust or crushed Oreo cookies)

Melt marshmallows in the milk over medium heat. While marshmallows are melting, break up candy bar.

When marshmallows are melted, add the candy bar. Stir well so marshmallows and candy bar don't stick to the bottom.

Once the mixture is melted and while it is cooling, beat the whipping cream. Add sugar to whipping cream to taste.

When chocolate mixture is cool, fold half or three-fourths of the whipping cream into the chocolate mixture. Keep the rest of the whipping cream for the top of the pie.

Add mixture to pie crust. Put remaining whipped cream on top and grate chocolate to finish the look.

If you want to be fancy, make this recipe and put it in parfait glasses.

Carol Lemley
Grass Valley, Oregon

Desserts: Pudding

Brown Sugar Pudding

2 c. water
1 c. brown sugar
2 Tbsp. butter, divided
½ c. milk
1 c. white sugar
1 c. flour

2 tsp. baking powder
½ tsp. salt
½ tsp. cinnamon
½ tsp. nutmeg

In an oven-safe pot, bring the water, brown sugar and 1 Tbsp. butter to a boil on the stove top. Mix the remaining ingredients in a bowl to make a batter.

Gently spoon the batter on top of the boiling brown sugar water until top is covered. Bake at 350 degrees for 25 minutes, or until top is golden brown. Let cool to set. Can serve warm with vanilla ice cream or fresh cream.

Bonnie White
Baker City, Oregon • Oregon Trail Electric Cooperative

Plum Pudding

½ c. butter
1 c. sugar
3 eggs, beaten
1 c. plum puree
1 c. flour
½ tsp. cinnamon
1 tsp. baking soda
¼ tsp. nutmeg
3 Tbsp. sour milk
Sauce:
1 c. plum puree
½ c. water
2 tsp. cornstarch
1 c. sugar
2 Tbsp. butter

Cream butter and sugar together until fluffy. Add eggs and 1 c. plum puree; mix well. Sift dry ingredients together and add alternately with milk. Pour into shallow 6-by-1¾-inch pan. Bake at 350 degrees for 20 to 30 minutes, until set. Cut into squares and serve hot with sauce. It is better served warm, but is also good cold.

To make the sauce, heat plum puree and water. Mix cornstarch and sugar. Pour a little hot liquid over it and stir constantly. Pour back into puree and cook until thickened, stirring constantly. Add butter.

This is a recipe that is called for at every Thanksgiving and Christmas family meal. It is one I created.

Barbara L. Rexford
Bonners Ferry, Idaho • Northern Lights

Rice Pudding

½ c. rice
1 c. water
1 qt. milk
½ stick butter
3 eggs
½ c. sugar
1 c. raisins
½ tsp. vanilla
3 Tbsp. sugar
1 tsp. cinnamon

Bring water to a boil and add rice. Boil for 7 minutes.

Add milk and butter. Stir. Bring back to boil, cover and cook for 1 hour, watching closely so liquid does not boil over or go dry and scorch.

Beat eggs and sugar together. Add raisins and vanilla.

Pour into rice, then sprinkle with sugar and cinnamon.

I am the third generation for this recipe and I have passed it down to my daughter and granddaughter. It is a family recipe and is much enjoyed and asked for at special dinners.

Geraldine Boswell
Lacon, Illinois

Desserts: Variety

Apricot Cheese Delight

1 large can apricots, drained and cut (save juice)
1 can crushed pineapple, drained (save juice)
1 large package orange Jell-O
Topping:
½ c. sugar
3 Tbsp. flour
2 Tbsp. butter
1 egg, slightly beaten
1 c. combined juice
1 carton whipping cream
Cheddar cheese, grated

Dissolve Jell-O in 2 c. hot water. Add pineapple and apricots. Add 1 c. of the juice and save 1 c.

Chill the Jell-O until firm.

For the topping, combine sugar and flour. Blend in beaten egg. Gradually stir in juice. Cook over heat until thick. Remove and add butter. Let cool.

Fold in whipped cream and spread over Jell-O. Cover with grated Cheddar cheese.

The recipe was given to me from the Campoy family 41 years ago. It was their family recipe. We have served it at get-togethers, picnics, holidays, company dinners or just because we are hungry for it!

Judy Bean
Harpster, Idaho • Idaho County Light and Power

Apricot Delight

2 15-oz. cans (or 1-qt. jar) apricots
1 c. whipping cream
1 tsp. vanilla
1 c. walnuts, chopped
1 c. miniature marshmallows
Apricot, cut in half

Drain cans or jar of apricots. After draining, puree in blender. Set aside.

Whip whipping cream. Add vanilla and sweeten to taste. Fold apricots into whipped cream and add walnuts and miniature marshmallows.

Garnish with apricot halves, if desired.

Roxanne Clough
Kamiah, Idaho • Idaho County Light and Power

Berry Dessert

½ lb. large marshmallows
½ c. milk
8-oz. carton whipped topping
2½ c. boysenberries (or similar fruit)
1 c. juice
⅓ c. plus ¼ c. sugar
2 Tbsp. cornstarch
1 Tbsp. lemon juice
1½ c. graham crackers
¼ c. butter, melted

Melt the marshmallows and milk in a double boiler. Cool. When cool, add whipped topping.

Combine boysenberries, juice, ⅓ c. sugar, cornstarch and lemon juice. Cook over low heat until thickened. Cool.

Crush graham crackers. Add butter and ¼ c. sugar; mix. Place in a 9-by-11-inch pan, reserving 2 Tbsp. for topping. Bake at 350 degrees for 8 minutes. Cool.

When cool, add half of the marshmallow mixture, a layer of berries and the rest of the marshmallow mixture. Top with the reserved crumb mixture. Chill.

This recipe has been in our family for at least 40 years. It is always asked for when we have a gathering.

Ruth Falk
Harrisburg, Oregon • Consumers Power

Char's Rhubarb Dessert

4 c. rhubarb, diced
2 c. strawberries (fresh or frozen)
1 c. sugar
1 package strawberry Jell-O
1 package white cake mix
1 c. water
⅓ c. butter, melted

Combine rhubarb, strawberries and sugar. Sugar can be reduced to ½ c., if desired. Spread mixture into 9-by-13-inch pan.

Sprinkle dry Jell-O over rhubarb mixture. Sprinkle cake mix over all. Pour water over all, then drizzle butter on top. Bake at 350 for one hour. Serve with whipped cream or vanilla ice cream.

Charmaree Cook
North Pole, Alaska • Golden Valley Electric Association

Choco Layer Delight

Crust:

1½ c. whole wheat flour
½ c. vegetable oil
2 Tbsp. sugar
½ c. chopped walnuts

Preheat oven to 375 degrees.

Mix all ingredients well. Pat out in 9-by-12-inch baking dish. Bake for 15 minutes. Allow to cool.

First layer:

8 oz. light cream cheese
1 c. powdered sugar
1 c. Cool Whip

Cream together the cream cheese and powdered sugar. Blend in Cool Whip. Spread in even layer over crust.

Second layer:

2 3-oz. packages sugar-free instant pudding mix
3 c. skim milk

Mix well with wire whip or electric mixer. Allow to thicken slightly. Spread in even layer over the cream cheese layer. Refrigerate until firm.

Topping:

Cool Whip
Shredded coconut
Chocolate shavings

Put a thin layer of Cool Whip over pudding layer. Garnish with shredded coconut or chocolate shavings, if desired. Refrigerate. Cut into squares for serving.

My daughter adapted this recipe for a 4-H foods contest. It quickly became a family favorite, especially for Easter and other special occasions.

Rita Durrell
Philomath, Oregon • Consumers Power

Crème Brulée

18 oz. heavy cream
4 oz. sugar
1½ tsp. vanilla
5 egg yolks

Place everything but yolks in a saucepan full of water, and bring to a moderate heat.

When hot, add 3 oz. cream to yolks, whipping constantly. While whipping, incorporate all of the yolk-cream to the rest of the cream. Ladle into ramekins. Place ramekins in a baking dish.

Pour hot water into the pan with the ramekins to a half-inch below the ramekins. Place in 350-degree oven and bake for 30 to 40 minutes, until non-jiggly. Remove from the oven and let rest in the water bath for 10 minutes; place in refrigerator. When serving, place sugar on top and flame torch.

Jim Angerman
Tillamook, Oregon • Tillamook PUD

Country Apple Dumplins

2 Granny Smith apples
2 packages canned crescent rolls
1½ c. sugar
1 Tbsp. cinnamon
2 sticks butter
1 can Mountain Dew

Cut each apple into 8 slices. Separate crescent rolls and wrap each apple slice in a roll. Pinch to seal.

Place in single layer in 9-by-13-inch glass baking dish.

Melt butter and mix with sugar and cinnamon. Pour or spoon over apples.

Pour Mountain Dew over all, and bake at 350 degrees for 35 to 40 minutes.

Note: May cut sugar to 1 c. if desired.

Elizabeth (Patsy) Miller
Southport, Florida • Gulf Coast Electric Cooperative

Grandma's Cherry Vareneki

5 c. flour
7 tsp. baking powder
½ tsp. salt
1 c. milk
1 c. sour cream
4 eggs
4 c. sweet cherries, pitted and cut in half
1 c. sugar
4 Tbsp. cornstarch

Combine flour, baking powder and salt. Make a well in the center of the dry ingredients. Combine milk, sour cream and beaten eggs; mix well. Pour into dry ingredients and stir to make a soft dough.

Roll out the dough on a well-floured surface to ¼-inch thick. Cut dough into approximate 4-inch squares.

Combine sugar, cornstarch and cherries. Put a spoonful of cherries in the center of each square. Fold in half and pinch edges together well.

Deep-fat fry at 350 to 360 degrees for 3 to 5 minutes. When golden brown, remove and drain on paper towel. Do not make too large or the center will not be done or warm. Only put together as you fry, otherwise they get too juicy and fall apart.

A family tradition when the Bing cherries are ripe. Of German origin.

Valerie Giesbrecht
Othello, Washington • Big Bend Electric

Health Candy

1 c. sugar, white or brown
1 c. half-and-half
1 c. white corn syrup
4 c. corn flakes
4 c. Rice Krispies
1 c. coconut
1 c. Spanish peanuts (others may be used)

To make a syrup, combine sugar, half-and-half and corn syrup. Boil to a soft ball stage. This takes longer than you think. While this is cooking, mix together in a large pan the corn flakes, Rice Krispies, coconut and peanuts.

Butter a 9-by-13-inch cookie sheet. When the syrup has reached the soft ball stage, pour over the cereal mixture until well mixed. Put in buttered pan. When cool, cut into squares.

This recipe has been in my family for some 70 years and it isn't Christmas without it. Also, it doesn't taste overly sweet!

Ruth Falk
Harrisburg, Oregon • Consumers Power

Mamaw's Black Diamond Dessert Ball

8 oz. cream cheese, softened
½ c. butter, softened (no substitutes)
¼ tsp. vanilla extract
¾ c. confectioners' sugar
2 Tbsp. brown sugar
1 c. miniature chocolate chips
1 c. chopped pecans

In a mixing bowl, beat the cream cheese, butter and vanilla until fluffy. Gradually add the sugars and beat until combined. Stir in chocolate chips. Cover and refrigerate for 2 hours.

Shape into a ball and roll in the chopped pecans.

Serve with graham crackers, animal crackers, vanilla wafers, pretzel sticks, etc.

Alma Osborne
Panama City, Florida • Gulf Coast Electric Cooperative

Pecan Bark

1 c. unsalted butter (no substitutes)
1 c. firmly packed brown sugar
1 c. pecans or walnuts, chopped (enough to lightly cover all the graham crackers)
24 chocolate graham cracker squares

Preheat oven to 350 degrees. Line a 10-by-15-inch cookie bar pan with aluminum and lightly butter the foil. Use butter, not oil or shortening, as it cooks into the grahams a little. (I haven't tried spraying with nonstick spray, but that should work and would lessen the calories.)

Place graham crackers on the cookie sheet in one layer; it should take exactly 24 pieces. Sprinkle the nuts evenly over the grahams and set aside.

Melt the butter in a saucepan. Add brown sugar and stir until the mixture boils. Boil for one minute only. Pour mixture evenly over the nuts/graham crackers. Bake for 10 minutes.

Remove from oven and put directly into the freezer. Leave in freezer for 1 hour, then take out and break into pieces. It doesn't need to be refrigerated, but we like it better when it is.

As a decoration, you can melt some white chocolate and put a small drizzle on the chilled pan. Return the pan to refrigerator for a few minutes to set the chocolate.

This stores well in the refrigerator for several weeks.

This is one of our favorite snack/desserts. I have made it on many occasions and am always asked to bring it.

Roxanne Jones
Pahrump, Nevada • Valley Electric Association

Sharon's Very Easy Christmas Fudge

3 c. semisweet chocolate chips
¼ c. butter
14-oz. can sweetened condensed milk
1 c. walnuts, chopped (optional)

Place chocolate chips, sweetened condensed milk and butter in a large microwaveable bowl. Zap in the microwave on medium until chips are melted, about 3 to 5 minutes, stirring once or twice during cooking. Stir in the nuts.

Pour into a well-buttered 8-by-8-inch glass baking dish (or double this recipe and use a 9-by-13-inch baking dish). Refrigerate until set and cut into squares.

Sharon Capovilla

Valentine Éclair Delight

3.4-oz. box French vanilla instant pudding mix (see cook's notes)
1 c. milk (see cook's notes)
1 8-oz. carton frozen whipped dairy topping, defrosted
½ box (7.5 oz.) graham crackers
1 c. prepared chocolate frosting (see cook's notes)

In a medium bowl, mix the milk and powdered pudding mix. Fold in the whipped topping to form about 4 c. pudding mixture, and set aside.

Place single layer of graham crackers in the bottom of an 8-by-8-inch glass or ceramic dish. Spread about 1 c. of the pudding mixture over the crackers. Top with another layer of crackers, and follow with another layer (1 c.) of pudding mixture. Continue until all pudding mixture is used, about four layers total (see cook's notes). Top with a final layer of crackers.

Spread the chocolate frosting over the top layer of crackers, sealing it to the edges of the dish. Cover the dish with plastic wrap and refrigerate at least 4 hours or up to 24 hours before serving.

Cook's notes:
- Do not prepare pudding mix before adding to recipe.
- Any type of milk (skim, low-fat or whole) will work.
- Depending on the size and brand of your crackers, you may have an additional graham layer. Try to create, by breaking the crackers on their perforations, an entire layer of cracker, then pudding mixture, so crackers form the bottom and top layers, with the pudding mixture sandwiched between each cracker layer.
- Leftover chocolate frosting can be covered and refrigerated for up to two weeks. Let refrigerated frosting sit at room temperature for at least 20 minutes before spreading.

Geraldine Smith
Tacoma, Washington • Elmhurst Mutual Power & Light

Main Dishes: Beef and Turkey

Barbecued Beef Brisket

Whole brisket
4 Tbsp. liquid smoke
1 Tbsp. garlic powder
1 Tbsp. celery salt
8 Tbsp. Worcestershire sauce, divided
1 large onion
1 stick butter
8 oz. tomato sauce
1 c. ketchup
½ c. brown sugar
½ c. vinegar

Rub or brush both sides of brisket with liquid smoke, garlic powder, celery salt and 4 Tbsp. Worcestershire sauce. Leave in refrigerator for 8 hours. Cook at 250 degrees for 8 hours.

Sauté onion in butter. Simmer with tomato sauce, ketchup, brown sugar, vinegar and 4 Tbsp. Worcestershire sauce.

Drain fat and remove excess fat from brisket. Add sauce and cook an additional 1 to 2 hours.

Charles Rossman

Beef Tomato

2 Tbsp. grapeseed oil
2 lbs. flank steak, sliced in thin strips across the grain
1 large white onion, sliced in strips
1 large bell pepper, sliced in strips
6 Roma tomatoes, sliced in wedges
2 tsp. oyster sauce
½ c. low-sodium soy sauce
½ c. water
2 tsp. sugar
2 Tbsp. cornstarch

In a bowl, mix oyster sauce, soy sauce, water, sugar and cornstarch. Set aside.

Heat oil in a large skillet or wok. Add steak and stir fry until just pink. Add onions and peppers. Continue to stir fry until onions start to soften. Add tomatoes and stir fry for an additional 3 minutes.

Stir the oyster sauce mix, then add it to the skillet. Continue to stir fry until the sauce thickens. Serve over rice.

Faye M. Pena
Willcox, Arizona • Sulphur Springs Valley Electric Cooperative

The Best Beef Stroganoff

2 lbs. boneless steak or good stew beef
Margarine, enough to brown meat
1 clove garlic, mashed
¾ Tbsp. salt
½ c. sour cream
1 c. chopped onions
1 to 2 c. water
2 bouillon cubes
3 Tbsp. flour
Dash of pepper

Brown meat in margarine. Add garlic, onion and seasonings. Add bouillon and cook until tender (very slow heat). Just before serving, add sour cream. Serve over noodles or rice.

Just let slowly cook and it will melt in your mouth. The secret is to let it simmer for hours and hours.

This recipe is 30 years old.

Vera Holman
Las Vegas, Nevada

Cheeseburg Egg Rolls

1 lb. ground beef
1 lb. Cheddar cheese, grated
1 package egg roll wrappers
Oil
Soy sauce, sesame seed oil or your favorite dipping sauce

Cook ground beef. Drain grease and cool slightly. Mix grated Cheddar cheese with ground beef. Use approximately ⅓ c. mixture per egg roll wrapper and roll according to directions on egg roll wrappers. Fry in oil and drain on a paper towel. Dip in bowls of soy sauce, sesame seed oil or your favorite sauce. They also are delicious without sauce.

These are good with raw bean sprouts added, but more difficult to roll.

This is my most-requested meal from family and others who have tried them.

Dawn Schutt
Susanville, California • Lassen Municipal Utility District

Chinese Hamburger Casserole

1 lb. hamburger, browned and drained
1 can cream of mushroom soup
1 can cream of chicken soup
1 c. chopped celery
½ c. chopped onion
½ c. uncooked white rice (not instant)
1 c. water
2 to 3 Tbsp. soy sauce
1 to 1½ c. chow mein noodles

Mix all ingredients except the chow mein noodles thoroughly. Bake, covered, at 350 degrees for 30 minutes.

Uncover and stir in the chow mein noodles. Bake uncovered for another 30 minutes.

Years ago I used to raft rivers a lot—followed by a potluck and pictures a week or two later. This recipe was given to me after my enthusing over it. Our family loved it. Our four children grew up with it and I still make it 40 year later.

Frances Whiteman
The Dalles, Oregon • Wasco Electric Cooperative

Dan's Chuck Wagon Surprise

1 lb. ground venison, elk or lean ground beef
3-oz. can pork and beans
1 green or red bell pepper, diced
1 small onion, diced
½ tsp. garlic salt

Fry meat, onion and bell pepper in a small amount of cooking oil until meat is brown and bell pepper cuts with a spoon.

Add pork and beans and garlic salt. Cook, stirring often, for about 5 minutes.

Dan Thies
Brookings, Oregon • Coos-Curry Electric Cooperative

Grandpa's Extra-Tender Meatloaf

2 lbs. ground beef
2 eggs
1 c. fine bread crumbs
1 tsp. soy sauce
1 Tbsp. lemon juice
¼ c. ketchup
2 Tbsp. minced onion
1 tsp. minced parsley
½ c. milk
2 tsp. margarine
1¼ tsp. salt

Combine beef, eggs, crumbs, soy sauce, lemon juice, ketchup, onions and parsley in a large bowl. Mix well with your hands. Add milk and beat with a fork (this makes the loaf light). Add salt; mix with fork. Firm into a loaf in a greased pan. Dot with margarine.

Bake at 350 degrees for about 1½ hours. Carefully drain off liquid from the pan halfway through baking.

Wende Blackburn
Lake Wales, Florida

Hamburger Casserole

12-oz. package egg noodles
2 lbs. ground beef
1 large onion, diced
1 small can tomato sauce
3 oz. cream cheese
1 c. sour cream
1 can cream of mushroom soup, undiluted
Salt and pepper, to taste
Cheese, grated (sharp Cheddar is best)

Cook noodles according to directions. Drain and place in bottom of casserole dish. Brown beef and onion; drain. Add tomato sauce. Spread mixture over noodles. Mix cream cheese, sour cream and cream of mushroom soup and spread over beef mixture. Sprinkle grated cheese on top.

Bake in a 350-degree oven enough to heat thoroughly, or heat in the microwave.

Nadine Hall
Pace, Florida • Escambia River Electric Cooperative

Haystacks

2 lbs. ground beef
½ small onion, chopped
1 c. ketchup
2 Tbsp. brown sugar
2 Tbsp. regular mustard
1 Tbsp. Worcestershire sauce
1 tsp. salt
1 tsp. pepper
2 to 4 Tbsp. horseradish
Crushed corn chips
Varied toppings (see below)
Cheese sauce:
¼ c. butter
¼ c. flour
2 c. milk
Shredded cheese, to taste

Cook beef and onion together until done. Add ketchup, brown sugar, mustard, Worcestershire sauce, salt, pepper and horse-radish. Place this mixture over crushed corn chips, such as tortilla chips.

Add to the top whatever you want. For instance: rice, pork and beans, chili beans, lettuce, chopped avocado, chopped tomatoes, hot sauce or salsa, olives, chopped lettuce, chopped celery, chopped onions, chopped green peppers, finely chopped jalapeno peppers or whatever is left over in the refrigerator that sounds good.

To make the cheese sauce, melt the butter. Add the flour, then add milk and cheese. Add milk or sour cream if necessary. Pour the cheese sauce on top of the haystacks.

Diane Elder
Paisley, Oregon • Surprise Valley Electrification

Margie Nitz Casserole

1 to 1½ lbs. lean ground beef
1 can vegetables (or frozen; I like green beans)
1 can mushroom soup
20 to 25 Tater Tots
½ c. Cheddar cheese, shredded

Spray baking pan. Place ground beef on bottom of baking pan. Pour on vegetables. Top with soup, covering all of the vegetables. Cover with Tater Tots. Bake 1½ hours at 375 degrees. Cover with cheese 10 minutes before it is done.

Another dish most people like—even my husband, who doesn't like casseroles.

Rose Lausman
Lake Placid, Florida • Glades Electric Cooperative

Mashed Potatoes and Beef and Green Bean Casserole

1½ lbs. ground round beef
2 Tbsp. Saffola oil
½ c. sweet onion, minced
4 to 5 cloves garlic, peeled and minced
Kosher salt, to taste
Fresh ground pepper, to taste
3 14½-oz. cans whole green beans, drained
2 11½-oz. cans tomato soup concentrate
6 to 8 Yukon Gold potatoes, washed and cut in quarters
4 Tbsp. butter
2 to 3 Tbsp. milk

Heat large skillet with oil to medium. Add ground beef, onions and garlic. Season with salt and pepper. Fry until meat is done and nicely browned. Drain off fat. Add soup and green beans; mix gently.

Spray a 9-by-13-inch casserole dish with cooking spray and add meat mixture.

In a separate saucepan, cover potatoes with water and bring to a boil. Cook for about 20 minutes, until tender. Drain water and add butter to melt. Start mashing, then add milk to desired consistency and mash until fluffy. Season with kosher salt and fresh cracked pepper.

Spoon mashed potatoes in big mounds on top of meat mixture evenly, forming peaks.

Preheat oven to 350 degrees and bake for about an hour, until nice and bubbly. Turn oven to broil and brown the peaks of the potatoes.

This was always the dinner I would ask my Mommy to make. Then, as my sisters and I got old enough, Mom taught us how to make it. Now, since years have passed and my folks are gone, we still keep our old family favorite alive by passing on the recipe to our fourth generation.

Heather Shuford
Nehalem, Oregon • Tillamook PUD

Pigs in a Blanket

1 large head cabbage
1 to 1½ lbs. ground beef
1 c. instant rice
½ c. onion, chopped
½ c. bell pepper, chopped
1 small can tomato sauce
Salt and pepper, to taste
1 to 2 cans diced tomatoes

Preheat oven to 350 degrees.

Boil whole head of cabbage. When soft enough, cut whole outer leaves. Continue boiling cabbage. As the leaves get soft, cut them off, continuing until the leaves are too small to wrap.

Mix ground beef, seasoning, rice, onions and tomato sauce in a bowl. As cabbage leaves get soft, wrap 1½ Tbsp. ground beef in leaves. Place close together in a casserole dish with wrapped side down. Once all are wrapped, add one or two cans of diced tomatoes over all of the wraps.

Bake for 2½ to 3 hours.

My mom would make these for us when we were kids.

Evelyn Earnshaw
North Pole, Alaska • Golden Valley Electric

Secret 'Old Settler's Bean' Recipe

½ lb. ground beef
¼ c. barbecue sauce
½ lb. bacon, cooked and chopped
2 Tbsp. prepared mustard
1 onion, chopped
1 tsp. salt
⅓ c. brown sugar
1 can red kidney beans, undrained
⅓ c. white sugar (optional)
1 can pinto beans, undrained
¼ c. ketchup
1 can butter beans, undrained
2 Tbsp. molasses
½ tsp. chili powder
½ tsp. black pepper

Brown the ground beef; add onion and sauté. Add bacon and mix the brown sugar, white sugar, ketchup, molasses, chili powder, black pepper, barbecue sauce, mustard and salt. Mix in the kidney, pinto and butter beans.

Place in a large casserole dish and bake at 350 degrees for 1 hour, stirring every 15 minutes.

Patty Albright
Neskowin, Oregon • Tillamook PUD

Steve's Brisket

6 to 8 lb. brisket (first cut; shrinkage about 25 percent)
3 cloves garlic, cut into slices
2 c. red wine (Chianti or any dry red wine)
1 package onion soup mix (dry)
6 carrots, cut into 1-inch pieces (optional)

Rinse brisket and dry with a paper towel. Cut 8 to 10 deep 1-inch slits in brisket (fatty side). Place 1 sliver of garlic into each slit. Place into glass or aluminum pan (lasagna size), fat side up, and cover with 1 c. wine.

Refrigerate, covered with foil, overnight. Seal edges tightly.

Remove from fridge. Add second cup of wine, onion mix, and carrots.

Reseal foil tightly. Cook at 300 to 325 degrees for 4 hours.

Remove from oven. Remove foil and let rest at least 15 minutes. Slice.

Stephen Harad
Lakewood Ranch, Florida • Peace River Electric Cooperative

Stuffed Turkey Burgers

1 lb. ground turkey
¼ c. quick-cooking oats
1 egg
½ tsp. garlic powder
Dash of pepper
½ c. onion, chopped
¼ c. pickle relish, drained
2 Tbsp. ketchup
2 tsp. mustard
Cheddar cheese slices
Lettuce (optional)
Tomato slices (optional)

Combine turkey, oats, egg, garlic powder and pepper. Divide turkey mixture in half. On two pieces of wax paper, shape each half of turkey mixture in a patty. Sprinkle with onions and relish, leaving ½-inch border around outside edges. Top with mustard and ketchup. Add cheese slice.

Carefully place remaining turkey mixture on top of cheese. Press turkey patty edges together to seal. Lightly grease a grill rack and place patties on grill. Season to taste.

Grill for 8 minutes per side. Serve on toasted buns.

Shar Lequerica
La Grande, Oregon • Oregon Trail Electric Cooperative

Tamale Loaf

1 medium onion, diced and sautéed
2 cloves garlic, minced and sautéed with the onion
1 lb. ground beef
1 c. milk
2 eggs
16-oz. can black olives, drained, cut in halves
16-oz. can whole kernel corn, drained
16-oz. can stewed diced tomatoes
2 c. yellow cornmeal
2 tsp. chili powder
2 tsp. Mrs. Dash
Salt and pepper, to taste

Combine all ingredients in a large mixing bowl. Mix thoroughly to even consistency. Pour into two ovenproof casserole dishes (one quart or larger size). Bake for 1 hour at 375 degrees.

This tamale loaf became a family tradition for New Year's Day over 50 years ago.

Rita Durrell
Philomath, Oregon • Consumers Power

Teriyaki Meatballs

1 lb. burger
2 Tbsp. oil
¼ c. chopped onion
3 tsp. sherry wine
¼ c. flour
½ c. water
1 egg
2 Tbsp. brown sugar
1 tsp. salt
⅛ tsp. ginger
¼ tsp. pepper
1 tsp. garlic salt
¼ c. soy sauce, divided
2 Tbsp. cornstarch

Combine meat, onion, flour, egg, salt, pepper and 1 Tbsp. of soy sauce. Shape mixture into meatballs. Heat oil and fry meatballs until lightly browned.

Combine rest of soy sauce, sherry, water, brown sugar, ginger, garlic salt and cornstarch.

Add meatballs and cook on low heat until sauce thickens. Can use a crock pot. Serve with rice.

Kathy Jones
Corvallis, Oregon • Consumers Power

Waikiki Meatballs

1½ lbs. lean ground beef
⅔ c. cracker crumbs
⅓ c. onion, minced
1 egg
1½ tsp. salt
1 Tbsp. shortening
2 Tbsp. cornstarch
½ c. brown sugar, packed
20-oz. can pineapple tidbits (reserve juice)
1 Tbsp. soy sauce
⅓ c. apple cider vinegar
⅓ c. green pepper, chopped

Combine beef, cracker crumbs, minced onion, egg and salt. Mix thoroughly and make into small balls. Melt shortening in a large skillet. Add meatballs; brown and cook thoroughly. Remove from heat and drain well.

In a medium bowl, mix cornstarch, brown sugar, reserved juice from pineapple, soy sauce and vinegar. Stir until completely dissolved. Pour mixture into skillet and bring to a slow simmer until it thickens.

Add meatballs to the mixture and heat until hot. Add green pepper and pineapple tidbits. Heat until warm. Serve over rice.

Audra Shrauger
Prineville, Oregon • Central Electric Cooperative

Yap Yap

1 lb. Chinese noodles, cooked
2 lbs. hamburger, browned
6 celery stalks, diced
1 green pepper, diced
1 dry onion, diced
1 can cream of chicken soup
1 can tomato soup
1 can vegetable soup
1 can sliced mushrooms, drained
1 can sliced water chestnuts, drained
1 can black olives, drained and sliced

Sauté the celery, green pepper and onion. Mix all ingredients together and put in a large greased casserole. Cover and bake for 1 hour at 350 degrees.

Dede Hurford
Newberg and Rockaway Beach, Oregon • Tillamook PUD

Main Dishes: Chicken

Aunt Ruth's Russian Chicken

1 whole chicken, cut up, or chicken breasts
16 oz. sour cream
1 envelope onion soup mix
3 Tbsp. Russian salad dressing

Place cut-up chicken in a 9-by-13-inch pan. Spread sour cream over chicken and sprinkle with soup mix. Drizzle with Russian dressing.

Cover with aluminum foil. Bake at 350 degrees for 1 hour, or until done. Serve over white rice.

Rosalva Lemmon
Prosser, Washington • Benton Rural Electric Association

Chicken and Biscuits

3 boneless, skinless chicken breasts, cooked
2 large cans cream of chicken soup
2 cans biscuits
Mixed vegetables, cooked (optional)

Preheat oven to 400 degrees.

Grease the bottom of a casserole dish. Shred cooked chicken and put it in the dish. Add cream of chicken soup and vegetables. Mix. Cover with foil and bake until boiling.

I cook my biscuits according to the package directions and then place them on top of the boiling casserole dish. My mom always laid her biscuits right on top of the casserole when it was hot and boiling, and then put it back in the oven to cook until biscuits were browned, 12 minutes or so. Either way works great.

This recipe was a family favorite with us kids when we were growing up. It's now one of my kids' favorite dishes.

Diana Glazebrook
Tucson, Arizona

Chicken Cacciatore

3-lb. fryer, cut up
3 Tbsp. shortening
2 medium onions, sliced
2 cloves garlic, minced
1-lb. can tomatoes
8-oz. can tomato sauce
⅓ c. green pepper, minced
1 tsp. salt

¼ tsp. black pepper
¼ tsp. cayenne pepper (optional)
1 tsp. ground oregano
½ tsp. crushed basil
½ tsp. celery salt (optional)
1 bay leaf
¼ c. Chianti wine (optional)

Brown chicken pieces in hot shortening in a skillet. Layer onion slices in slow cooker. Put browned chicken on top of onion slices and add remaining ingredients. Cover and cook on low for 6 to 8 hours or on high for 3 to 4 hours. Discard bay leaf.

Serve chicken with sauce over buttered spaghetti or rice.

Linda Hunt
Susanville, California • Lassen Municipal Utility District

Chicken Enchiladas

1 onion, chopped
¼ c. margarine
¼ c. flour
2½ c. water
1 Tbsp. chicken seasoning
8 oz. sour cream
3 c. chicken, cooked and finely chopped
2 c. Cheddar cheese, shredded
3 tsp. taco seasoning
½ c. salsa
¼ c. sliced ripe olives (optional)
10 to 12 flour tortillas
Lettuce, shredded
Tomatoes, chopped

In medium saucepan, cook onion in margarine until tender. Stir in flour and cook until bubbly. Add water and chicken seasoning. Cook and stir until thickened. Remove from heat and add sour cream.

In a large bowl, combine 1 c. of the sauce with chicken, 1 c. of the cheese, taco seasoning, salsa and olives.

Place ⅓ c. of filling on each tortilla. Roll up and place seam side down in a greased 9-by-13-inch baking pan. Spoon remaining sauce over top. Sprinkle with the rest of the cheese. Bake at 350 degrees for 30 to 40 minutes.

Serve with lettuce and tomatoes. Top with additional salsa.

Delicious and brings many cheers when served at our house.

Malinda Schrock
Litchfield, California • Plumas-Sierra Rural Electric Cooperative

Chicken Enchiladas

3 chicken breasts, cubed
½ c. onion, chopped
2 Tbsp. butter
2 tsp. steak seasoning
1 tsp. Italian seasoning
½ tsp. salt
½ tsp. pepper
½ c. medium salsa
1 can black beans, drained and rinsed
1 c. sour cream
2 c. Cheddar cheese, shredded
8 medium-size flour tortillas
1 can cream of chicken soup
3 Tbsp. fresh basil, chopped

Melt butter in a skillet. Cook chicken and onion with the steak seasoning, Italian seasoning, salt and pepper until chicken is no longer pink and onions are transparent.

Add salsa and beans to chicken mixture. Remove from heat and set aside.

Grease a 9-by-13-inch dish. Spread the cream of chicken soup in the bottom of the dish. Spread about ⅛ c. of sour cream down the center of a tortilla, add about the same amount of shredded cheese, and then scoop about ½ c. of chicken mixture on top.

Without tucking the ends, roll the tortilla and place in pan. Repeat until tortillas are gone. Top with any remaining cheese and basil.

Bake at 350 degrees for 30 minutes. Serve with sour cream, salsa and a side of Spanish rice.

Chelsea Scilzo
Dillingham, Alaska • Nushagak Cooperative

Chicken Enchiladas

3 c. cooked chicken, chopped bite size
1 can cream of chicken soup
1 can cream of mushroom soup
16 oz. sour cream
8-oz. can chopped green chilies
2 c. Monterey Jack cheese (save some for topping)
¼ c. chopped onions
Diced jalapenos (to desired hotness)
Dash of garlic
1 Tbsp. cilantro
10 to 12 flour tortillas
Paprika

Mix all ingredients and spoon into the center of each tortilla. Roll up and place in a greased 9-by-13-inch baking pan. Pour remaining mixture over top of enchiladas.

Cover top with extra cheese and some chopped onions. Sprinkle top with paprika.

Bake at 375 degrees for 25 minutes, until bubbly.

Mickye Sheidler
Panama City, Florida · Gulf Coast Electric Cooperative

Chicken Stroganoff

5 boneless chicken breast halves, skinned
    and cut into 1-inch pieces
Black pepper or lemon pepper
3 Tbsp. butter
1 medium onion, thinly sliced
½ pound mushrooms, sliced
1 Tbsp. flour
1½ c. chicken broth
1 Tbsp. Dijon mustard
1 tsp. basil
1 Tbsp. parsley
½ c. sour cream
Salt and pepper, to taste

Season the chicken with lemon pepper. Melt 2 Tbsp. butter in heavy skillet over medium heat. Add chicken and cook until opaque, stirring occasionally. Transfer to a dish and keep warm.

Add onion and mushrooms to skillet and cook until light brown, stirring frequently. Add chicken back to skillet.

Melt remaining butter in a small saucepan, add flour and stir for 3 minutes. Whisk in broth and other seasonings. Stir in sour cream. Heat sauce until warm; do not boil. Pour over chicken. Serve with rice or pasta.

Ruth Keller
Redmond, Oregon · Central Electric Cooperative

Chicken Supreme

4 boneless, skinless chicken breasts
1 package cream cheese, softened
4 bacon strips, cooked
26-oz. can cream of mushroom soup
Bread crumbs
1 egg
1 c. milk
1 c. flour
Deep fry oil

Mix egg and milk together.

Fillet chicken breasts in half. Pound until tender, then cut into strips 2 to 3 inches wide.

Spread cream cheese on chicken breasts. Place half of a piece of cooked bacon on chicken and roll up. Secure with toothpick.

Heat deep fry oil. Place rolled-up chicken in seasoned flour, then in egg/milk mixture. Roll in bread crumbs.

Put in hot oil and cook until golden brown and chicken is done. Place on paper towel and remove toothpicks.

Put in baking pan. Cover with soup mixed with additional milk. Cover and bake at 350 degrees for 30 minutes.

Serve over spiral noodles or rice.

Ed Riepma
Bend, Oregon

Chicken Tikka Masala

3 to 4 chicken breasts
Marinade:
1 c. plain yogurt
1 Tbsp. garam masala
2 Tbsp. lemon juice
Sauce:
2 Tbsp. butter
1 large onion
3 Tbsp. garam masala
1 tsp. ground ginger
2 tsp. salt
2 Roma tomatoes, diced
1 can diced tomatoes
½ can tomato paste
1 c. cream
4 cloves garlic
½ bunch cilantro
Sugar, to taste

Cut chicken into bite-size pieces, then marinate at least 1 hour or overnight in yogurt with garam masala and lemon juice. Remove chicken from marinade and place on baking sheet with foil and bake at 325 degrees until juices run clear, about 25 minutes.

To make sauce, sauté onion and garlic in butter. Add salt, garam masala and ginger and sauté 1 minute. Add tomatoes and tomato paste and simmer until tender. Add sugar to taste. Add all to blender and puree to desired texture, then return to pan and add chicken, cream and cilantro.

Serve with basmati rice and naan.

Tamara Tuttle
Gold Beach, Oregon • Coos-Curry Electric Cooperative

Mexican Chicken

1½ lbs. chicken, cooked and shredded (or 2 cans)
16 oz. green sauce
12 corn tortillas
16 oz. sour cream
¼ c. chopped onion
1 can cream of chicken soup
1 can cream of mushroom soup
Cheddar cheese
Monterey Jack cheese
16-oz. can chicken broth (or less for thicker)

Cut tortillas into 1-inch strips. Combine sour cream, soups, broth and onion and stir to blend. In a 10-by-15-inch casserole dish, spray the bottom with oil and layer half of the tortilla strips on the bottom. Top with half the chicken, then half the combined soup mixture, and half of the cheeses. Repeat layers. Cover and let set overnight.

Preheat oven to 325 degrees. Cook covered for 1 hour, then uncovered for a half hour.

I have a friend that makes this with broccoli and doesn't let it sit overnight, and says it is still good.

Gretchen Browne
Carnation, Washington • Tanner Electric

Oooooooh! Chicken Rice Casserole

2 c. (16) chicken nuggets, cut into smaller pieces
1 c. Uncle Ben's Ready Rice - Garden Vegetable
   (one microwavable bag)
1 c. celery, chopped
1 c. french fried onions (dried)
1 can cream of chicken soup
½ c. mayonnaise
¼ c. milk
2 Tbsp. margarine, melted

Preheat oven to 325 degrees.

Microwave the chicken nuggets and rice according to the package directions. Combine them with all of the other ingredients, except the margarine, in a large bowl.

Mix carefully, but completely.

Pour the mixture into a 1½-quart casserole. Pour the melted margarine over the mixture.

Bake for 30 minutes. Serve.

You can substitute plain cooked chicken or turkey for the nuggets and plain cooked rice for the microwaved rice.

Kathleen Houge
Vancouver, Washington • West Oregon Electric Cooperative

PopPop's Chicken

1 whole chicken
Teriyaki sauce, 1 whole batch per chicken (see recipe below)
2 scallions, sliced into whatever length desired

Rinse chicken and pat dry with paper towels. With a pastry brush, coat chicken inside and out with teriyaki sauce. Add scallions at this point or part way through cooking.

Put the chicken in a roasting pan and roast for about 1 hour for a 3.5-lb. bird, or longer for a larger bird. Baste every 15 minutes. If you want a darker bird, baste more frequently. Chicken is done when juices from the leg run clear when pierced with a knife. Allow chicken to rest for 20 minutes before carving.

Teriyaki sauce:

1 c. shoyu (Japanese soy sauce)
1 c. sugar
3-inch piece fresh ginger, peeled and sliced
4 cloves garlic, peeled and minced

Stir together shoyu and sugar in a small saucepan over low heat until sugar dissolves, about 2 minutes. Add ginger and garlic. Simmer for about 30 minutes, stirring occasionally.

Debi Rossman

Portobello and Chicken and Rice

1 can Progresso Recipe Cooking Sauce
   (creamy portobello mushroom)
1 can cream of mushroom soup
1 c. sour cream
2 medium portobello mushrooms, cut into chunks
1 tsp. kosher salt
¼ tsp. pepper
6 chicken breasts
2 Tbsp. butter
Salt and pepper, to taste
2½ c. rice

Place cooking sauce, soup, sour cream, kosher salt and pepper in a medium pot. Heat on low for about 45 minutes, or until hot. Stir constantly.

Place butter in a frying pan and brown chicken with salt and pepper. Once browned, place in an oven-safe dish. Bake for 30 to 45 minutes at 300 degrees.

Cook rice per package directions.

Place a piece of chicken on a plate and put one or two scoops of rice alongside. Cover chicken and rice with cooking sauce. Serve.

Daniel Tovrea
La Pine, Oregon • Midstate Electric

Southern Fried Chicken

1 whole chicken
Milk
Salt
Pepper
Garlic powder
Oil
Gravy:
3 to 4 Tbsp. flour
1 c. water
1 c. milk

Cut up chicken and wash well. Soak in milk for 15 minutes. Remove from milk and drain on paper towels.

Sprinkle each piece with salt, pepper and garlic powder. Roll each piece in flour and fry in 1 inch of hot oil until golden brown.

To make gravy, pour off excess grease and brown flour in the drippings with enough of the oil to absorb the flour. Add salt and pepper, to taste. Quickly whisk water and milk together and cook until thickened.

Esther Gore
La Pine, Oregon • Midstate Electric

Stuffed Chicken Breasts

6 chicken breasts, pounded to lay flat (I put the chicken
   in a large Ziploc bag and pound it with a hammer)
1 box chicken stuffing mix
½ c. butter, melted
¾ c. white cooking wine
¼ c. low-sodium soy sauce
Flour

Prepare stuffing following box directions; let cool. Place about ¼ c. of stuffing in center of chicken breast, roll the chicken breast around the stuffing and then roll in flour.

Place seam side down in a buttered casserole pan. Place in a 400-degree oven for 30 minutes.

While chicken is baking, mix white cooking wine with soy sauce. After the 30 minutes of baking, lower oven to 350 degrees. Pour the mixture over the chicken. Bake another 45 minutes, basting every 15 minutes.

A super delicious and savory recipe from my mom that I now make. Everyone loves them and always requests I make them for the next dinner party.

Jennifer Davis
Bend, Oregon • Pacific Power

Yummy Chicken Asparagus Casserole

4 medium-sized skinless, boneless chicken breasts
2 Tbsp. salad oil
10½ oz.-can cream of chicken soup
⅓ c. mayonnaise
1 tsp. lemon juice
½ tsp. curry powder
⅛ tsp. pepper
10-oz. package frozen asparagus, thawed
¼ c. Cheddar cheese, grated

Preheat oven to 375 degrees.

Cut chicken breasts into 1-inch strips. In a large skillet over high heat, cook chicken in hot oil until lightly browned. Remove from heat.

In a small bowl, mix soup, mayonnaise, lemon juice, curry powder and pepper.

Place half of asparagus in bottom of a 1½-qt. casserole dish. Top with half of the soup mixture and all of the cooked chicken. Layer remaining asparagus and soup mixture. Top with grated cheese.

Bake for 30 to 35 minutes.

Trina Smith
Noti, Oregon • Blachly-Lane Electric Cooperative

Main Dishes: Eggs

Breakfast Burritos

4 10-inch flour tortillas
1 Tbsp. margarine
¼ c. green pepper, chopped into small pieces
¼ c. onion, chopped
8 eggs or equivalent egg substitute
½ tsp. salt
¼ tsp. pepper
Small bag shredded Mexican cheese
½ c. salsa

Melt margarine in a large pan. Add onions and peppers. Cook for 1 minute over medium heat.

In a bowl, beat eggs, salt and pepper together. Pour eggs into pan, stirring frequently, until eggs are cooked.

Place the tortillas on plates and divide the scrambled egg mixture evenly in the center of tortillas. Top with cheese and salsa. Fold into burrito form.

Charlotte Robson
Bradenton, Florida • Peace River Electric Cooperative

Breakfast Casserole

Large bag Tater Tots
8 to 10 eggs
Bacon, cooked; ham, cut into chunks; or
    sausage, cooked and chopped
Onion powder, to taste
Green chilies (optional)
Salt and pepper, to taste
Cheese

Thaw the Tater Tots. Crumble them and press into the bottom of a well-greased baking dish.

Beat eggs and pour over the top of Tater Tots. Add bacon, ham or sausage. Add onion powder and/or green chilies and salt and pepper, to taste. For holidays, use green and red peppers and chop them up very small. Looks great to serve Christmas morning.

Layer the top with a cheese of your choice.

Bake at 350 degrees for about one hour. Check with a tooth-pick to see if it is done. Cut into squares.

This is a family favorite. We have it Christmas morning. It cooks while we open gifts. My kids and grandkids love it.

Diana Glazebrook
Tucson, Arizona

Eggs and Sausage Casserole

8 eggs, lightly beaten
1 c. milk
1 c. sharp Cheddar cheese, grated
6 to 8 slices bread, cubed
1 lb. sausage, browned, crumbled and drained
1 tsp. dry mustard, optional

Mix all ingredients. Pour into greased 9-by-12-inch casserole dish. Set in refrigerator overnight.

Bake in a 350-degree oven for 30 minutes. Serve for breakfast or as a side with fish.

Nadine Hall
Pace, Florida • Escambia River Electric Cooperative

Fried Egg Sandwiches

2 slices whole wheat bread
2 large eggs
2 slices thick bacon
1-oz. slice mozzarella cheese
Mayonnaise

Spread both slices of bread with a small amount of mayonnaise. Cook and drain the bacon. Whip the eggs with a fork, and pour into a small amount of hot oil in a frying pan. Cook on one side, flip over and cook on other side.

Place the bacon on the bread and lay the slice of cheese over it. Place eggs on top, cover with remaining slice of bread, and cut sandwich in two pieces. If your horses are saddled and you haven't time to wait, you can wrap it in foil, stick it in your pocket, and eat on the go.

Sharon Livingston
Long Creek, Oregon • Oregon Trail Electric Cooperative

Jim's Mexican-Style Baked Eggs

1 c. canned refried beans
1½ Tbsp. water
5 scallions (use green tops)
1 10-oz. package frozen spinach, thawed and drained
⅓ c. sour cream
1 c. hot pepper cheese
4 large eggs
½ c. mild salsa
4 flour tortillas
1 c. prepared guacamole
Dash of pepper

Preheat oven to 400 degrees. Mix the beans and water in a greased 8-by-8-inch baking dish or four small individual baking dishes. Mix the spinach and all but 2 Tbsp. of the scallions. Spread on top of the beans. Top with sour cream and cheese.

Make four indentations in the surface, or one each if using individual baking dishes. Break an egg into each hole. Spoon the salsa on top and bake, uncovered, for 20 minutes or until eggs are set. Heat the tortillas in the microwave and serve alongside in a basket.

When the eggs are done, spoon ¼ c. of guacamole on top, then sprinkle the pepper and remaining scallions over all.

Jim Angerman
Tillamook, Oregon • Tillamook PUD

Omelet in a Bag

Eggs
Cheese, grated
Ham, diced
Onion, diced
Green pepper, diced
Tomato, diced
Frozen hash browns
Salsa
Bacon, cooked
Sausage, precooked

Guests for breakfast—or a late-night snack? Here is an easy, fun way to prepare a tasty treat. It's a great conversation piece and everyone gets involved in the process.

Have your guests use a permanent marker to write their name on a quart-size self-locking freezer bag.

Crack two large or extra-large eggs into each bag (more than two will not work). Shake, mixing them well.

Have the guests add the prepared ingredients of their choice to the bag and shake. Don't put in too many hashbrowns—they take over. Make sure to get the air out of the bag and zip it up.

Place the bags into boiling water for exactly 13 minutes. You can usually cook six to eight omelets in a large pot. For more, make another pot of boiling water.

Open the bag and the omelet will roll out easily.

Aileen Benson
Sutherlin, Oregon

Main Dishes: Lamb and Pork

Baby Bone-In Lamb Chops

4 baby lamb chops
2 cloves garlic
¼ c. Italian parsley, chopped
Salt and pepper, to taste
⅛ c. Italian olive oil
1 lemon
Iceberg lettuce (cold)

In a medium frying pan, heat olive oil over medium heat. Add garlic. Place chops in pan and add parsley. Cover pan and brown one side of the chops. Turn chops and brown again. Add ½ c. water and uncover pan. Cook until water mostly evaporates.

Squeeze half of the lemon over the chops while in the pan. Add salt and pepper, to taste.

Place petals of lettuce on a plate. Squeeze remaining lemon on lettuce. Drizzle more olive oil on lettuce, then place pork chops on top of lettuce.

Edmond Torrillo
Panama City, Florida • Gulf Coast Electric Cooperative

Black Cherry Ham with Cherry Compote

2 c. water
6 oz. black cherry-flavored gelatin (use ¼ c.)
½ tsp. cinnamon
¼ tsp. nutmeg
¼ tsp. ground cloves
9 star anise, reserve 5 to decorate
15-oz. can dark sweet pitted cherries, in heavy syrup
½ c. raisins
¼ c. dried cranberries
1 Tbsp. frozen orange juice concentrate
2 Tbsp. balsamic vinegar
5- to 6-lb. bone-in ham, fully cooked
15 to 20 whole cloves, depending on ham size

In a medium saucepan, combine ¼ c. gelatin, cinnamon,

nutmeg, ground cloves and 4 star anise. Stir in water and bring to a boil. Reduce heat and simmer 5 minutes, stirring occasionally. Remove ½ c. glaze to small bowl and set aside.

To saucepan, stir in cherries, raisins, cranberries, orange juice concentrate and balsamic vinegar. Stir and simmer 7 to 10 minutes, until raisins and cranberries are plump. Drain off ¾ c. juice and reserve for final brush when ham is cooked. Set aside. Refrigerate compote until ready to use.

Preheat oven to 325 degrees.

Score top and sides of ham. Using a sharp knife, make a diamond pattern about 2 inches apart. Stud the centers with cloves. Place ham in a roaster pan on a rack. Add 1 c. water to the bottom of the pan. Brush top, sides and all exposed ham with reserved glaze. Cover and cook for 15 minutes per pound.

Remove from oven and brush with reserved ½ c. juice from compote. Decorate with reserved star anise.

Let rest 10 minutes before slicing. Serve 2 Tbsp. compote with each serving, or on the side.

My holiday ham we make for gatherings has become my family and friends' favorite!

Peggy Calhoun
Portland, Oregon • PGE

Cabbage with Sausage

1 small to medium head cabbage
1 lb. rope-style sausage
2 c. mustard sauce (recipe below)
3 Tbsp. bacon bits

Preheat oven to 350 degrees.

Cut cabbage into 1-inch thick slices, discarding core. Place in a saucepot. Salt lightly if desired, and bring to a boil. Cook only to tender-crisp stage (do not overcook) and remove from heat. Drain well. Place in a 5-quart Dutch oven, or an ovenproof 3-quart casserole that is at least 3 inches deep.

Cut sausage into 1½-inch chunks and spread over cabbage. Set the casserole in the oven while you make mustard sauce. Pour sauce evenly over cabbage and sausage.

Sprinkle with bacon bits and return to oven. Bake, uncovered until heated through, 30 to 35 minutes.

Mustard sauce:

4 Tbsp. butter or margarine
4 Tbsp. flour
½ tsp. salt
2 c. milk
2 to 3 Tbsp. prepared mustard

Melt butter in saucepan. Blend in flour and salt. Cook over low heat, stirring until smooth and bubbly. Stir in milk and heat to boiling, stirring constantly. Cook about 1 minute. Remove from heat and stir in mustard.

Note: Sauce may be made in microwave, substituting a 1-qt. Pyrex measuring cup for saucepot, and following above procedure. Milk must be stirred in with care, or preheated, to avoid breaking glass measuring cup. Add milk to 2 c. mark on measuring cup. Heat and stir at high power, in intervals, until boiling. Mixture must boil well before adding sauce, or it will curdle.

Wini Whitaker
Redmond, Oregon • Central Electric Cooperative

Chorizo Cordell

1 lb. chorizo
1 package rapid-rise yeast
½ c. onion, chopped
1½ c. hot water
2 cloves garlic, chopped
2 tsp. butter, softened
1½ c. white flour
½ lb. Monterey Jack, cubed
½ c. whole wheat flour
7-oz. can diced green chilies, drained
½ c. cornmeal
1 large egg, beaten
1 Tbsp. sugar
3 tsp. sesame seeds
½ tsp. salt

Remove chorizo from casings and slice or crumble into a large skillet. Add onion and garlic and sauté, stirring occasionally, until chorizo begins to brown. Drain, if necessary, and set aside to cool.

In a large bowl, combine white flour, whole wheat flour, cornmeal, sugar, salt and yeast. Stir in hot water and butter. Mix well. Cover and let rest for 10 minutes. Grease a 9-inch or 10-inch springform pan.

Stir down dough. With buttered fingers, press two-thirds of the dough into the bottom of the pan. Add cheese and chilies to the chorizo mixture. Spoon the mixture into the center of the dough. Leave a rim of dough around the edge.

Drop remaining dough by tablespoon over the filling. With buttered fingers, spread dough over the filling. Cover and let rise 30 minutes.

Heat oven to 400 degrees. Brush dough with egg and sprinkle with sesame seeds.

Bake for 30 minutes, then cool for 5 minutes. Remove sides of pan. To serve, cut into wedges.

Joni Cordell
Tensed, Idaho • Clearwater Power Co.

Mama Flynn's Chinese Rice Casserole

1 lb. pork sausage
1 c. instant rice
2 medium onions, chopped
1 tsp. salt (optional)
1 c. celery, chopped
½ tsp. black pepper
2 small cans chicken with rice soup
1 can sliced water chestnuts
1 can water
Slivered almonds (optional)
Soy sauce

Boil onion and celery until tender, but still crisp, or zap in the microwave. Drain.

Fry sausage. Crumble and drain any grease.

In a 9-by-13-inch casserole, place rice, celery-onion mixture and sausage. Add soup, water, seasonings and water chestnuts. Top with a sprinkling of slivered almonds.

Bake uncovered for 30 minutes, or cook in microwave 8 to 10 minutes.

Serve with soy sauce.

Patty Albright
Neskowin, Oregon · Tillamook PUD

One Dish

1 large head cabbage, cut up
2 lbs. green beans
1 bone-in ham

Preheat oven to 350 degrees. Cook ham for one hour. Add cabbage and beans and cook together for one hour.

Sometimes I just put everything in the oven at once and cook altogether.

My son loves this dish. I have to make it every time I visit.

Evelyn Earnshaw
North Pole, Alaska · Golden Valley Electric

One Pot Bean and Sausage Meal

1 lb. dry white beans
8 oz. macaroni
1 onion
1 lb. sausage
1 clove garlic
15-oz. can cut-up tomatoes
¾ c. dark corn syrup
1 tsp. parsley
1 tsp. oregano
Salt and pepper, to taste

Soak beans overnight. Drain, reserving 2 c. juice. Brown sausage, onion and garlic. Add macaroni, syrup, tomatoes, beans with juice and seasonings. Heat on low/medium until macaroni is done.

Leslie Welker
Lyle, Washington · Klickitat PUD

Oven BBQ Ribs

1 rack baby back ribs, sliced into individual sections
1 c. ketchup
⅓ c. Worcestershire sauce
1 tsp. chili powder
½ tsp. salt
2 dashes Tabasco sauce
1½ c. water

Layer ribs on their side in a glass casserole pan. Bake for 25 minutes at 400 degrees. Pour off grease.

Mix together the remaining ingredients for the sauce and add to ribs. Lower the oven to 325 degrees and bake for 1½ hours, basting ribs every 15 minutes. Add more water if the sauce gets too thick.

My mom made these for our family and friends. They were a huge hit. Very delicious. I am carrying on the tradition now since my mom has passed.

Jennifer Davis
Bend, Oregon · Pacific Power

Pork Chop Dinner

1 lb. pork chops
4 medium potatoes, peeled and thinly sliced
1 medium onion, thinly sliced
1 tsp. dry mustard
½ tsp. ground black pepper
1 tsp. paprika
1 tsp. seasoning salt

¼ c. butter, melted

Mix together the dry mustard, pepper, paprika and seasoning salt.

Preheat oven to 350 degrees. Butter a large baking dish. Layer half of the potatoes and half of the onions. Sprinkle with half of the seasonings. Layer with half of the chops. Layer the rest of potatoes and onions. Sprinkle with the remaining seasonings and layer with the rest of the chops.

Pour butter over top. Cover and cook for 1 hour.

Shirley J. Tumbush
Panama City, Florida

Pork with Apple Gravy

4 to 6 lean boneless pork loin chops, fat trimmed
    (about ½-inch thick or thicker)
Dashes of Worstershire sauce
Sprinkle of garlic powder
Sprinkle of onion powder
Sprinkle of sage powder
Sprinkle of paprika
Sprinkle of black pepper
2 Tbsp. oil or bacon drippings
1 c. flavored bouillon or broth
1 medium onion, halved and sliced thinly (if you
    prefer, cut the slices in half again)
1 stalk celery, finely chopped (leaves are good, too)
1 small whole apple, cored and chopped
    finely (or half of one large apple)
2 Tbsp. flour
2 heaping Tbsp. plain yogurt or sour cream
Salt and pepper, to taste

Lightly sprinkle Worstershire sauce on both sides of chops, then sprinkle with garlic, onion powder, sage, paprika and black pepper. In large skillet or Dutch oven, brown chops in hot oil on both sides, about 15 minutes total.

Add ½ c. broth (reserve other ½ c.), onion and celery. Cover and simmer 50 to 60 minutes, or until tender. Remove chops to covered glass dish to keep warm.

To Dutch oven, slowly stir in 2 Tbsp. of flour and cook over low heat, stirring constantly, until thickened. Stir in apples and yogurt or sour cream; cook and stir until thoroughly heated. If a thinner gravy is desired, add some of the reserved broth. Pour over chops and serve with your favorite veggies and grains.

Lin Howard
Alturas, California • Surprise Valley Electrification

Sally's Easy Pork Casserole

1 can mushroom soup
1 can mushrooms
1 package thin pork chops or steaks
1 package chicken Stove Top dressing
½ c. milk
1 onion, chopped
Salt and pepper, to taste

In a saucepan, stir together mushroom soup and milk. Heat to boil. Stir in onion and mushrooms. Remove from heat.

Spray a casserole dish with cooking spray. Add a layer of pork and sprinkle with salt and pepper. Add soup mixture.

Make Stove Top stuffing as directed on box. Spread over the top of the soup mixture. Top with foil.

Bake at 350 degrees for 1 hour. Remove foil and bake for 15 minutes.

Sally Hays
Orofino, Idaho

Sausage-Filled Crepes

Crepes:
3 eggs, beaten
1 c. plus 1 Tbsp. milk
1 c. flour
½ tsp. salt

Combine ingredients, beating until smooth. Fry in light olive oil at 275 degrees until firm. Use a scant ¼ c. for each.

Fillings:
1 lb. sausage
¼ c. onion, chopped
½ c. Cheddar cheese, shredded
3-oz. package cream cheese
¼ tsp. dried marjoram

Combine sausage with chopped onion. Fry until done. Drain. Add remaining ingredients.

Topping:
½ c. sour cream
¼ c. butter, softened

Place 2 Tbsp. of filling down center of each crepe. Roll up. Place in a greased 7-by-11-inch baking dish. Cover and chill. Bake at 375 degrees for 40 minutes. Spoon topping over hot crepes and bake uncovered for 5 to 10 minutes.

Transgenerational favorite. Grandchildren, children and grandparents.

Joan Grossel
Lakewood Ranch, Florida • Peace River Electric Cooperative

Sausage Pizza

¼ c. oil

1 egg

2 Tbsp. sugar

1 tsp. salt

½ c. hot water

1 Tbsp. yeast

½ c. warm water

3 c. flour

1 tsp. oregano

1½ lb. sausage, fried

Pizza sauce

Onions, chopped

Peppers

Mushrooms

Olives, optional

Cheese, shredded

Beat together oil and egg. Add sugar and hot water. Dissolve yeast in warm water and add to first mixture. Add oregano and salt, then add flour. Knead well. Put dough lump on a greased pan; cover with a cloth and let it rise for 30 minutes.

Press out the dough and spread on pizza sauce. Layer on sausage and vegetables. Sprinkle with cheese. Bake at 375 degrees until done.

Our family loves this pizza. When the ladies are gone for the day, the boys enjoy making it for dinner.

Kathy Schrock
Litchfield, California • Plumas-Sierra Rural Electric Cooperative

Sausage-Spinach Quiche

2 deep-dish pie crusts

1 tsp. oil

1 lb. seasoned pork sausage

¼ c. onion, chopped

4 eggs, beaten

2 pkgs. creamed spinach

6 Tbsp. milk

1 c. mushroom slices, drained (optional)

1½ c. Swiss cheese, shredded

Salt and pepper, to taste

Preheat oven to 400 degrees.

Brown pork sausage and onion in oil. In a large bowl, combine the sausage and onion with the eggs, spinach, milk, mushrooms, cheese, salt and pepper. Mix well. Divide the mixture and pour into the two pie crusts.

Bake for 30 to 40 minutes. When done, cool for at least 20 minutes before slicing.

This recipe makes two quiche; however, one can be frozen for later use. Thaw before baking.

Aurora Leveroni
Graeagle, California • Plumas-Sierra Rural Electric Cooperative

Spiced Pork Chops with Honey and Grapes

2 Tbsp. butter or olive oil

3 or 4 boneless pork loin chops, cut 1 to 1¼-inch thick

Flour

3 Tbsp. honey

1 Tbsp. cinnamon

4 whole cloves or ¼ tsp. ground cloves

2 tsp. ground ginger

1 c. seedless grapes

Salt and pepper, to taste

Preheat oven to 325 degrees.

Dredge chops with flour, shaking off excess. In an ovenproof pan, heat oil or butter. Brown chops to golden brown. Remove from heat.

Add remaining ingredients, distributing over and around the pork chops. Salt and pepper to taste.

Cover and place in oven for 45 minutes. Remove from oven; do not lift the lid. Let the pan rest for 15 to 20 minutes.

Serve, spooning the pan juices with grapes over the chops.

Bill Rhoads
Brookings, Oregon • Coos-Curry Electric Cooperative

Slow Cooker Maple Chipotle Pulled Pork

5-lbs. pork loin or shoulder roast

½ tsp. powdered ginger

1 Tbsp. freshly ground black pepper

1 Tbsp. dry thyme

1 Tbsp. garlic powder

1 Tbsp. paprika (I prefer smoked)

1 to 2 tsp. chipotle powder (to taste)

1 tsp. ground cumin

½ tsp. ground cinnamon

1 Tbsp. sea salt (optional or to taste)

Combine the dry ingredients to make a rub. Pat the pork dry with paper towels. Rub the spice mixture all over the pork. Let sit while you prepare the base.

Base:

1 medium-sized onion, chopped

3 cloves garlic, minced or thinly sliced

4 medium-sized firm apples, peeled and chunked

½ to 1 tsp. ground chipotle powder, according to taste

¼ c. apple cider vinegar

2 Tbsp. chopped fresh thyme (or 1 tsp. dry thyme)
1½ c. chicken stock
¼ c. maple syrup
Sea salt and ground pepper, to taste

Place the onions, garlic and apples in an even layer in the slow cooker. Combine chipotle powder, vinegar, thyme, maple syrup, sea salt and pepper in a small bowl and whisk together. Pour over the onion mixture, followed by the stock.

Place the rubbed roast in the slow cooker. Cover and cook until the pork is fork tender, about 6 to 8 hours on high or 8 to 10 hours on low.

While the pork is cooking, make the maple chipotle sauce.

Maple Chipotle Barbeque Sauce:

In a small saucepan, cook slowly over medium low heat until well softened and beginning to caramelize:

3 Tbsp. olive oil
3 cloves garlic, chopped
1 medium red onion, chopped
Add:
2 c. plain tomato sauce
¼ c. maple syrup
¼ c. apple cider vinegar
1 to 2 tsp. ground chipotle powder, to taste
1 tsp. black pepper
½ tsp. ground dry thyme
1 tsp. sea salt

Simmer slowly for 20 to 30 minutes, or until reduced by about one-fourth, stirring often. When cool, puree in a blender or food processor until smooth. Makes about 2½ c.

Turn off the slow cooker and remove the pork to a cutting board. Using two forks, shred the meat into bite-sized pieces, discarding any large pieces of fat. Add the sauce to the shredded meat, and mix to combine. Serve on your favorite rolls or buns.

Carrie Falotico
Lebanon, Oregon • Consumers Power

Main Dishes: Pasta

Baked Lasagna

2 Tbsp. butter
1 large onion, chopped
1½ lbs. ground beef
14.5-oz. can sliced stewed tomatoes
8-oz. can tomato sauce
1 Tbsp. oregano
1 tsp. salt
¼ tsp. pepper
1 tsp. onion salt
8-oz. package lasagna noodles
2 c. cottage cheese
1 c. Parmesan cheese, grated
5 c. mozzarella cheese

Sauté onions in melted butter. Add beef and brown. Drain off fat. Add stewed tomatoes, tomato sauce and seasonings. Simmer, uncovered, for 30 minutes.

Cook noodles according to package and drain.

Place one-third of sauce mixture in bottom of a 9-by-13-inch baking dish. Top the sauce layer with half of the noodles. Layer half of the cottage cheese over the noodles. Top with half of the Parmesan cheese and half of the mozzarella cheese. Repeat these layers, ending with the tomato-sauce mixture.

Bake at 350 degrees for 20 to 25 minutes. Let stand for 10 minutes before serving. It can be prepared the day before and baked just before eating.

Everyone in my family loves this dish and it has become our yearly Christmas Eve tradition.

Mary Rider
Monroe, Washington

Baked Spaghetti

1 c. onion, chopped
1 c. green pepper, chopped
1 Tbsp. butter or margarine
28-oz. can petite diced tomatoes with liquid
4-oz. can mushroom stems and pieces, drained (or fresh mushrooms)
2¼-oz. can sliced ripe olives, drained
2 tsp. dried oregano
1 lb. sausage, browned and drained
12 oz. spaghetti, cooked and drained
2 c. Cheddar cheese, shredded
10¾-oz. can condensed cream of mushroom soup, undiluted
¼ c. water
¼ c. Parmesan cheese, grated

In a large skillet, sauté onion and green pepper in butter until tender. Add tomatoes, mushrooms, olives and oregano. Add meat. Simmer, uncovered, for 10 minutes.

Place half of the spaghetti in a greased 9-by-13-inch baking dish. Top with half of the vegetable mixture. Sprinkle with 1 c. of Cheddar cheese. Repeat layers.

Mix the soup and water until smooth, and pour over the casserole. Sprinkle with Parmesan cheese. Bake uncovered at 350 degrees for 30 to 35 minutes, or until heated through.

Anna Free
Fairbanks, Alaska • Golden Valley Electric Association

Cleto Macaroni

1 box of pasta (rigatoni, mostaccioli or similar)
1 large onion, sliced
Butter or olive oil
2 to 3 cloves garlic, sliced
Cheese, grated (preferably a sharp Cheddar
   or Romano; the stouter the better)
Parmesan cheese
Garlic salt
Pepper

As the pasta cooks, fry the onion in butter or olive oil until it is golden brown. Just before the onion is ready, add the garlic.

When pasta is al denté, layer the pasta in a large bowl. Sprinkle with grated cheese and Parmesan cheese, garlic salt and pepper.

After the pasta is layered in the bowl (usually two or three layers), pour browned onions/garlic over the top.

A recipe passed down through the generations from our friend Cleto Yacomella, who was an Italian bachelor who lived here on East Fork.

Cheryl Baker

Grandma Mary's Easy Chicken Sausage and Veggie Lasagna

1¼ lbs. ground spicy Italian chicken sausage
2 Tbsp. white wine (to deglaze pan)
1 lb. white mushrooms, sliced
4 to 6 cloves garlic, peeled
1 shallot, peeled
⅓ sweet onion, peeled
¼ c. fresh basil leaves, chopped
25-oz. jar organic pasta sauce
26 oz. Pomi chopped tomatoes
¼ c. olive oil
½ tsp. kosher salt
¼ tsp. fresh ground pepper
½ tsp. sugar
3 small zucchini, sliced in rounds
2 c. fresh baby spinach leaves
2 c. fresh arugula leaves
15 oz. ricotta cheese, part skim
5 oz. Stella fresh grated 3-cheese Italian mix
16 oz. "no boiling" lasagna noodles

Heat large skillet with 1 to 2 Tbsp. olive oil on medium heat. Add chicken sausage. Fry until nicely browned and cooked through. Set aside on plate.

Deglaze pan with white wine and add mushrooms. Sauté until just starting to brown. Set aside with chicken.

Mince garlic, shallot and onion together. Add 1 Tbsp. of olive oil to pan with garlic mix. Sauté until soft. Add pasta sauce, tomatoes with the juices, ¼ c. olive oil, chicken sausage, mushrooms, basil leaves, salt, sugar and pepper. Simmer on low for an hour.

To assemble lasagna, spray large casserole with cooking spray, then ladle a little of sauce on the bottom. Then layer:

1 layer of noodles, side-by-side; sauce; zucchini, in flat layer; light sprinkle of Italian cheese mix; second layer of noodles; all of the spinach leaves; sauce; little spoonfuls of ricotta all over sauce; third layer of noodles; sauce; all of the arugula leaves; light sprinkle of Italian cheese mix; fourth layer of noodles; remaining sauce to cover top; all remaining cheese to cover top.

Bake in preheated oven at 350 for about 1 hour and 15 minutes, until bubbly and brown on top.

This one of my family's very favorite dinners that came from my Great-Grandma Mary, who lived to be 106 years old. The recipe now has some modern touches to make it fast and easy to make. All the generations in our family love this dinner, and we continue to pass the recipe on.

Heather Shuford
Nehalem, Oregon • Tillamook PUD

Japanese Noodles

1 lb. hamburger
8 to 10 oz. spaghetti noodles, cooked
½ c. onion, chopped
1 or 2 green peppers, chopped
1 c. carrots, chopped
1 head cabbage
1 tsp. garlic powder
1 tsp. Accent
½ tsp. salt
½ tsp. pepper
2 to 3 tsp. curry powder
2 Tbsp. soy sauce
¼ c. vegetable oil

Brown beef and add spices to taste. Add vegetables and cook until tender. Add noodles, oil and soy sauce. Mix all together and serve.

This recipe was given to me by my daughter-in-law. It was given to her by the cook from her high school in the small town of Terry, Montana. She scaled it down a bit.

Mary Cornelia
Casa Grande, Arizona • Electrical District No. 2

Lasagna

8 lasagna noodles
8 oz. light sour cream
1 to 1½ lbs. ground turkey sausage
¼ c. light cottage cheese
¼ tsp. garlic powder
6 green onions, chopped
24 oz. tomato sauce
8 oz. mozzarella cheese, grated
8 oz. light cream cheese
8 oz. Cheddar cheese, grated

Preheat oven to 350 degrees. Boil noodles al denté. Brown sausage, adding the garlic powder and tomato sauce just before it is done cooking.

In a bowl, mix the cream cheese, sour cream, cottage cheese and green onions. In a 9-by-13-inch pan, put down a layer of noodles, sausage and sauce mixture, cream cheeses, and sprinkle with mozzarella and Cheddar cheeses. Repeat with second layer.

Bake at 350 degrees for 30 minutes. Let cool slightly to set.

Gretchen Browne
Carnation, Washington • Tanner Electric

Low-Fat Macaroni and Cheese

1½ c. skim or 1-percent milk
2 c. Cheddar cheese, shredded
1 c. fat-free cottage cheese
¼ tsp. pepper
¼ tsp. salt
4 c. cooked macaroni
1½ Tbsp. onion, grated
Paprika

Mix first four ingredients in a blender. Stir into macaroni and onion. Place in lightly greased casserole dish and sprinkle with paprika. Bake at 350 degrees for 45 minutes.

Kathryn Folsom
Palmer, Alaska • Matanuska Electric Association

Million Dollar Spaghetti

7 oz. thin spaghetti
1 Tbsp. butter
1 lb. ground beef
1 lb., 13-oz. can Hunts tomato sauce
8 oz. cream cheese
1 c. sour cream
8 oz. cottage cheese
⅓ c. scallions, chopped
1 Tbsp. green pepper, minced
2 Tbsp. butter, melted
Salt and pepper, to taste

Cook spaghetti and drain. Sauté beef in butter until brown. Add tomato sauce, salt and pepper and remove from heat.

In a bowl, combine cheeses, sour cream, scallions and green pepper.

Take half of the spaghetti and place it in a 2-qt. casserole dish. Spread the cheese mixture over the noodles.

Add the balance of spaghetti and drizzle melted butter over noodles. Pour on the meat sauce.

Bake for 45 minutes at 350 degrees.

Dish can be refrigerated before baking, but remove 20 minutes before baking.

A perpetual request each time we visit the creator, my sister.

Paul Kraus
Marathon, Florida • Florida Keys Electric Cooperative

Soup Can Spaghetti

1 can tomato soup
1 can cream of mushroom soup
1 to 1½ lbs. ground beef
1 medium onion, chopped
2 Tbsp. vegetable oil
½ tsp. Tabasco sauce
½ tsp. chili powder
1 package spaghetti noodles

Sauté the onions until golden brown. Add the ground beef; stir until brown and done. Drain the grease. Add soups, Tabasco sauce and chili powder. Cook all for about 10 minutes, until hot and bubbly. Meanwhile, cook the spaghetti in a large pan until done and drain, then add the noodles to the sauce mixture. Serve with garlic bread or Parmesan cheese.

This recipe does very well if leftovers are eaten the next day. It tastes better that way.

Nancy Storlie
Fairbanks, Alaska • Golden Valley Electric

Sour Cream Noodle Bake

10 to 12 oz. noodles
1½ lbs. lean ground beef
¼ tsp. pepper
¼ tsp. garlic salt
1 c. tomato sauce
½ c. chopped onion
1 c. sharp Cheddar cheese
1 c. cottage cheese (fat free can be used)
1 c. sour cream (light sour cream can be used)

Cook noodles in salted boiling water until tender. Drain noodles well. Brown meat; add garlic salt, pepper, onion and tomato sauce. Simmer 10 minutes.

Combine sour cream, cottage cheese and noodles. Mix well. Put in a 9-by-13-inch casserole, alternating in layers, noodles then meat, etc. Top with Cheddar cheese. Bake at 350 degrees for 25 to 30 minutes.

The unbaked casserole freezes nicely. If freezing, hold off on placing the cheese on top until ready to bake.

This is a family favorite and the kids like it as well.

Leanne Hockman
Bend, Oregon • Central Electric Cooperative

Spaghetti Pie

1 lb. hamburger
1 medium onion, chopped
1 small can mushrooms
½ bell pepper, chopped
1 can Del Monte pasta sauce or 1 jar Ragu sauce
½ tsp. oregano
1 tsp. Italian seasoning
1 tsp. thyme
½ tsp. marjoram
1 tsp. salt
1 tsp. garlic
½ tsp. pepper
1 small package spaghetti
1 large tub cottage cheese
2 c. cheese, grated
1 pack American cheese slices

In a large frying pan, brown hamburger. Drain. Add onion and sauté. Add the next 10 ingredients. Cook until peppers are tender. Simmer for 10 minutes, without a lid. Add 1 tsp. salt to a pot of water and cook spaghetti. Drain.

In a casserole dish, add layer of spaghetti, layer of cottage cheese, layer of grated cheese, layer of sauce, layer of spaghetti, layer of cottage cheese and layer of sauce. Top with sliced American cheese.

Bake at 350 degrees until cheese is melted.

Sally Hays
Orofino, Idaho

Tina's Lasagna

1 lb. Italian sausage
1 lb. ground beef
1-plus clove garlic, minced
1 Tbsp. whole dry basil
1 tsp. salt
29-oz. can diced petite tomatoes
2 6-oz. cans tomato paste
6 wide lasagna noodles
⅓ c. Parmesan cheese
2 Tbsp. parsley flakes
3 eggs, beaten
½ tsp. pepper
1 tsp. salt
1 lb. mozzarella cheese

Preheat oven to 375 degrees. Brown both meats, then slowly drain. Add next 5 ingredients. Simmer, uncovered, for 30 minutes, stirring occasionally. Cook noodles in boiling salted water until tender; drain and rinse.

Combine remaining ingredients except mozzarella cheese. Place half of the noodles in a baking dish, spread half of the egg mixture, than half of the mozzarella cheese, then half of the meat sauce. Repeat.

Bake at 375 degrees for 30 minutes. Let stand for 10 minutes before cutting into squares. If refrigerated beforehand, cook an additional 15 minutes.

If you want to use ricotta cheese, add 3 c. with the egg mixture, minus one egg.

Tina Mintmier
Roseville, California; and Clio, California • Plumas-Sierra Rural Electric Cooperative

Main Dishes: Seafood

Easy and Healthy Shrimp Scampi

4 tsp. olive oil
1¼ lbs. medium shrimp, peeled and deveined (tails left on)
6 to 8 garlic cloves, minced
½ c. low-sodium chicken broth
½ c. dry white wine
¼ c. fresh lemon juice
¼ c. plus 1 Tbsp. parsley, minced
¼ tsp. salt
¼ tsp. freshly ground pepper
4 lemon wedges

In a large nonstick skillet, heat the oil. Sauté the shrimp until just pink, about 2 to 3 minutes. Add the garlic and cook, stirring constantly, about 30 seconds. With a slotted spoon, transfer the shrimp to a platter and keep warm.

In the skillet, combine the broth, wine, lemon juice, ¼ c. parsley, salt and pepper; bring to a boil. Boil, uncovered, until the sauce is reduced by half.

Spoon the sauce over the shrimp. Serve garnished with lemon wedges and sprinkled with the remaining parsley.

Jill Luoma
Mentor, Ohio • Florida Keys Electric Cooperative

Easy Tasty Shrimp

3 Tbsp. butter, divided
1 Tbsp. olive oil
Salt and pepper, to taste
1 clove garlic, cut in 4 pieces
2 Tbsp. onion, finely chopped
2 lbs. shrimp, precooked and peeled
¼ tsp. parsley flakes

Start with a preheated skillet (cast iron is best) over low heat. Melt 2 Tbsp. butter on low heat. Add olive oil and increase to medium heat. Don't burn.

Add shrimp, salt and pepper. Cook for 1 to 2 minutes. Stir shrimp. Add garlic and onion. Add the remaining butter and cook for 1 to 2 more minutes. Remove skillet from heat and let sit for 15 minutes.

Reheat to serving temperature. Remove garlic pieces before serving. Sprinkle parsley flakes over shrimp and serve.

Serving suggestions: as an appetizer; great over brown rice or with pasta; chill, remove tails, chop and add to tossed salad.

Garry Pitzer
Youngstown, Florida

Imitation Crab Enchilada with Green Sauce

½ c. and 2 Tbsp. canola oil
¾ lb. imitation crab meat
2 Tbsp. flour
2¼-oz. can sliced ripe olives, drained
19-oz. can green chili enchilada sauce
1¼ lb. Jack cheese, grated (reserve ½ c. for garnish)
2 Tbsp. green onions, chopped for garnish
12 corn tortillas

Preheat oven to 350 degrees.

Spray a 9-by-13-inch baking dish with cooking spray.

In a medium fry pan, heat 2 Tbsp. oil and add flour. Stir to allow flour to brown slightly. Add sauce and cook until it bubbles, about 3 minutes. Remove from heat.

In another fry pan, heat ½ c. oil over medium heat. Using tongs, dip tortillas one at a time in the oil. Let excess oil drip, then place tortilla in sauce. Remove and place tortilla on dish.

Sprinkle each tortilla with crab, cheese and a few olive slices. Roll tortilla, and place seam down in prepared baking dish. Place two layers in the dish.

Spread leftover enchilada sauce over the enchiladas. Cover with reserved ½ c. cheese and any sliced olives. Sprinkle with green onions.

Bake for 20 to 25 minutes, until bubbly and hot.

Note: Originally I ate these enchiladas with real crab meat, but to save money, I came up with the idea of substituting the real crab meat with imitation crab meat. My family noticed no difference at all.

Suzanne Duran
Janesville, California • Plumas-Sierra Rural Electric Cooperative

Roasted Salmon

½ c. orange juice
3 Tbsp. fresh lemon juice
3 tsp. grated lemon zest
2 Tbsp. brown sugar
4 tsp. chili powder
1 tsp. ground cumin
½ tsp. salt
½ tsp. lemon pepper
Pinch cayenne pepper
4 to 6 salmon fillets
Preheat oven to 400 degrees.

Oil shallow baking dish. Mix orange juice, lemon juice and zest, cumin, brown sugar, salt, lemon pepper and cayenne pepper together.

Place salmon in prepared dish. Pour mixture together over salmon. Turn to coat each side.

Roast 15 minutes.

Serve with sliced lemons and tartar sauce.

Dede Hurford
Newberg and Rockaway Beach, Oregon

Shrimp Monterey

2 garlic cloves, minced
2 Tbsp. butter
2 pounds uncooked medium shrimp, peeled and deveined
½ c. white wine or chicken broth
2 c. Monterey Jack cheese, shredded
2 Tbsp. minced fresh parsley
In a skillet over medium heat, sauté garlic in butter for 1 minute. Add shrimp; cook 4 to 5 minutes, or until pink. Using a slotted spoon, transfer shrimp to a greased 11-by-7-inch baking dish. Set aside and keep warm.

Add wine or broth to the skillet and bring to a boil. Cook and stir for 5 minutes, or until sauce is reduced. Pour over shrimp; top with cheese and parsley.

Bake, uncovered, at 350 degrees for 10 minutes, or until cheese is melted.

Geraldine Smith
Tacoma, Washington

Spicy Hot Garlic Shrimp

2 Tbsp. margarine
1 lb. shrimp (26 to 30), peeled and deveined
2 Tbsp. grapeseed oil
3 Tbsp. Sriracha hot sauce
6 to 8 cloves garlic, minced
⅓ c. sake (rice wine)
Melt margarine in a large skillet with grapeseed oil over medium-high heat. When the margarine is melted and blended with oil, add minced garlic. Fry quickly just to infuse flavor. Be careful not to burn the garlic.

Add shrimp and stir fry until just pink, but not cooked through. Add Sriracha and sake, and continue to stir fry until shrimp is done. Serve over hot rice or as an appetizer.

This dish does not call for salt, because it gets its salt from the margarine. Adding salt will make this dish too salty.

Faye M. Pena
Willcox, Arizona • Sulpher Springs Valley Electric Cooperative

Stuffed Calamari

1½ lbs. cleaned calamari (bodies and tentacles)
¼ lb. raw shrimp, chopped
¼ lb. scallops, chopped
¼ c. dry white wine
2 eggs, beaten
1 Tbsp. onion, chopped
½ c. flavored bread crumbs
1 Tbsp. butter, melted
¼ c. Italian parsley, chopped
3 cloves garlic, finely chopped
4 Tbsp. olive oil
4 Tbsp. Parmesan cheese, grated
¼ tsp. black pepper
Tomato sauce
Mix all ingredients to a pasty form.

With small spoon, stuff bodies three-fourths full. Lightly fry bodies on medium heat, along with tentacles. Roll and turn bodies for approximately 12 minutes.

Add the tomato sauce and let simmer for 1½ hours.

Served over fettuccine or linguini, and make your favorite garlic bread.

Edmond Torrillo
Panama City, Florida • Gulf Coast Electric Cooperative

Sushi Cake

2 c. uncooked sushi rice
½ c. rice vinegar
4 Tbsp. sugar
1 tsp. salt
1 avocado
2 oz. cream cheese, at room temperature
½ Tbsp. lemon juice
2 Tbsp. mayonnaise
2 large eggs, beaten
8 oz. smoked salmon
7 or 8 leaves fresh spinach

Rinse rice several times in running water until water is clear. Drain in a colander. Cook in a saucepan with a lid or rice cooker according to package directions. Use just a little bit less water than package directions so the rice is cooked a little bit harder.

While rice is cooking, combine rice vinegar, sugar and salt in a small bowl. Mix well.

In a lightly oiled fry pan, pour the beaten eggs and stir with a fork quickly and constantly to make finely scrambled eggs.

Halve avocado. Scoop out avocado pulp and mash in a bowl. Add cream cheese and mayonnaise. Mix well.

When rice is done, transfer to a medium bowl. Add rice vinegar mixture and mix gently. Don't stir too much. Let cool.

Line a 6-inch cake pan with plastic wrap and put scrambled eggs on the bottom. Then put half of the sushi rice. Flatten rice with a spatula (wet with water). Then put the avocado cream cheese mixture on the sushi rice, and place the rest of the sushi rice. With a wet spatula, press hard to settle. Let stand for 30 minutes, or until it sets.

In the meantime, make rose-shaped smoked salmon. Cut each piece of smoked salmon into a half-inch length. Piece by piece, use your fingers to roll up a rose to the size you want to create. Make 5 to 6 roses.

Turn the cake pan upside down onto a plate. Remove plastic wrap. Put the rose-shaped salmon and spinach leaves on top.

Hidemi Walsh
Plainfield, Indiana · Duke Energy

Salads

Armenian Salad

1 package chicken Rice-A-Roni
½ bell pepper
2 jars marinated artichoke hearts, chopped
2 bunches green onions, tops only, chopped
½ c. mayonnaise
¼ tsp. curry powder

Cook rice as directed on package except do not use butter to brown the rice. Let the rice cool.

Add remaining ingredients and mix. If more moisture is needed, add oil from the artichoke hearts.

Carol Huber
Oakridge, Oregon · Lane Electric

Aunt Wilma's Three-Bean Salad

15-oz. can green beans
15-oz. can yellow waxed beans
15-oz. can kidney beans
1 large white onion, chopped
½ c. apple cider vinegar or Zinfandel wine
1 green pepper, sliced (optional)
¼ c. salad oil or olive oil
¾ tsp. salt
¾ c. sugar
1 tsp. prepared mustard

Drain liquid from canned beans. In a large bowl, combine all ingredients. Refrigerate overnight before serving.

This easy, delicious recipe has been in my family for as long as I can remember, originally from my great aunt Wilma. Always requested at family get-togethers and a big hit at potlucks.

Judi Miller
Goldendale, Washington · Klickitat PUD

Bountiful Salad

Romaine, butter and red leaf lettuce
1 c. celery, diced
1 c. carrots, shredded
1 c. garbanzos, cooked and drained
¼ c. green onions, chopped
2 avocados, peeled and sliced
12 or more cherry tomatoes, halved
1 lb. fresh Dungeness crab meat
Thousand Island dressing:
1 c. mayonnaise
⅓ c. ketchup
2 tsp. lemon juice
2 Tbsp. sweet pickle relish
½ tsp. onion powder
½ tsp. garlic powder

Into a large bowl, tear bite-sized pieces of washed and patted-dry romaine, butter, and red leaf lettuce. Add remaining ingredients. Toss and serve with Thousand Island dressing.

To make the dressing, mix the ingredients well and store covered in the refrigerator.

Three generations devoured this salad served by my mother-in-law, Ethel Schaefer, at her family gatherings.

Lynne Schaefer
Sunriver, Oregon • Midstate Electric Cooperative

Broccoli Salad

3 stalks broccoli, cut into pieces
2 Tbsp. sweet onion
¼ lb. bacon, cut into small pieces and cooked
   to the crisp stage; pat grease off
1 c. grated Cheddar cheese
1 c. dried sweet cranberries
Dressing:
½ c. mayonnaise or Vegenaise
¼ c. sugar
3 Tbsp. white wine vinegar

Put the broccoli and onion through a food processor. Add bacon, cheese and cranberries.

Shake the dressing ingredients well to mix. Combine with broccoli mixture and chill at least 2 hours to let flavors blend.

This is a family favorite and a must at all family gatherings.

Diane Elder
Paisley, Oregon • Surprise Valley Electrification

Chinese Chicken Salad

½ head of cabbage, finely shredded
¼ c. scallions
½ lb. chicken breast, sautéed and cubed
1 package chicken-flavored ramen noodle mix
½ c. cashews or pine nuts
Dressing:
⅓ c. olive oil
¼ c. sugar
¼ c. cider vinegar
1 tsp. soy sauce
1 tsp. sesame oil
Chicken flavor packet from noodles

Crush noodles in the package; open and remove the flavor packet. Mix the noodles with the nuts and spread out on a baking pan. Brown under a broiler for a few minutes.

Mix together dressing ingredients. Toss all ingredients in a large bowl. Refrigerate for a few hours. Toss before serving.

This great salad has been served here many times and is a crowd pleaser.

Paul Kraus
Marathon, Florida • Florida Keys Electric Cooperative

Cold Carrot Salad

5 c. cooked carrots, cut into circles
1 green pepper, cut into strips
1 tsp. black pepper
1 large onion, cut into rings
1 can tomato soup
1 c. sugar
¾ c. apple cider vinegar
½ c. vegetable oil
1 tsp. Worcestershire sauce

Cook carrots until soft; drain. Add green pepper and onion.

Combine rest of the ingredients and beat with a mixer. Pour over carrots and refrigerate overnight.

Drain off sauce before serving.

Rosemary Hart
Casa Grande, Arizona • Electrical District No. 2

Cranberry Salad

1 lb. fresh cranberries, ground
1 bag marshmallows
¼ c. sugar
2 Golden Delicious apples, cut into bite-sized pieces
2 Gala apples, cut into bite-sized pieces
1 c. red grapes, cut in half
1 c. green grapes, cut in half
1 c. nuts, chopped
1 c. whipped cream, measured before you whip

Combine cranberries, marshmallows and sugar. Store in the refrigerator overnight.

The next day, add apples, grapes, nuts and whipped cream. Mix together.

Marlene Hostetler
Springfield, Oregon

Cranberry Salad

6 oz. package cherry Jell-O (or any berry flavor)
1¼ c. boiling water
1 lb. whole cranberries, frozen
1 c. crushed pineapple, drained
1½ c. miniature marshmallows
1½ c. sugar
½ pint whipping cream

Dissolve Jell-O in boiling water. Chill until slightly thickened, to a syrup consistency. Grind cranberries using a food processor or blender. Add pineapple, marshmallows and sugar. Chill the cranberry mixture.

Whip cream until stiff. Add mix to the Jell-O. Fold in the whipped cream. Chill for several hours until set.

Years ago, I was given this cranberry salad recipe by my mother. It has been a favorite of mine for years and now my two sons make it for Thanksgiving and Christmas for their families.

Jane Walter
Priest Lake, Idaho

Curried Chicken Salad

4 chicken breasts, skinless and boneless
2 c. seedless red grapes, halved
2 c. celery, sliced
1 c. slivered almonds, toasted
Dressing:
½ c. mayonnaise
½ c. poppy seed dressing
1½ tsp. curry powder

Bring a pot of salted water to a boil. Add chicken and boil until cooked through. Let cool in the fridge, then cut into ½-inch cubes. While the chicken is cooking, toast almonds in 350-degree oven until light brown, about 15 minutes.

Place chicken, grapes, celery and almonds in a large bowl. Combine dressing ingredients and pour over chicken mixture. Stir until combined. If it is a little dry, add additional poppy seed dressing until desired consistency. Serve over lettuce leaves.

This is always requested by my daughter for her birthday. Even though it's a cold salad, and her birthday is in October, the whole family enjoys it.

Trina Harris
Sandpoint, Idaho • Northern Lights

Grandma Galluzzo's Overnight Salad

1 head lettuce, shredded
½ c. green onions, sliced
1 c. celery, sliced
1 package frozen peas
2 c. mayonnaise (maybe a little less so salad is not soupy)
½ c. Parmesan cheese
1 tsp. seasoned salt
½ tsp. garlic salt
Tomatoes, chopped or sliced
½ lb. bacon, fried crisp and crumbled
1 hard-boiled egg, grated

Layer the first eight ingredients. Cover and refrigerate overnight.

Before serving, gently toss. Sprinkle the top with tomatoes, bacon and hard-boiled egg.

Lori Linville
La Pine, Oregon • Midstate Electric

Holiday Salad

1 large box raspberry Jell-O
2 c. boiling water
1 can crushed pineapple, undrained
1 apple, cored
1 orange, seeds removed
2 stalks celery
½ c. pecans
1 lb. cranberries

Dissolve Jell-O in boiling water. Pour in pineapple.

Grind cranberries, whole apple, whole orange, celery and pecans. Add to Jell-O and pineapple. Refrigerate overnight.

Esther Gore
La Pine, Oregon • Midstate Electric

Horseradish Salad

1 large box or 2 small boxes lime Jell-O
1 large box or 2 small boxes lemon Jell-O
1 large can crushed pineapple
1 can evaporated milk
2 Tbsp. creamed horseradish
1 c. mayonnaise
1¼ c. cottage cheese
½ c. chopped walnuts (optional)

Combine lemon and lime Jell-O with 2 c. boiling water in a large bowl. Stir for 2 minutes until dissolved completely. Do not add cold water. Place in the fridge and let it jell slightly.

After jelled slightly, take out of the fridge and mix in the rest of the ingredients with electric beater. Pour into a 9-by-13-inch dish and place back in the fridge. When firm, cut into squares. This can be used for a salad or dessert.

Mary LaSalle
North Pole, Alaska • Golden Valley Electric

Joanne's Potato Salad

10 lbs. russet potatoes
18 eggs
1 qt. sweet pickle relish
Mayonnaise
Yellow mustard
Garlic powder, to taste (about 2 to 2½ tsp.)
Onion powder, to taste (about 2 to 2½ tsp.)
2 tsp. celery seed
2 medium cans sliced black olives, drained

Cut potatoes into about 2-inch pieces, leaving the peel on. Boil potatoes until they are cooked to where you put a knife into the potato and it breaks in half. Remove from the stove and drain thoroughly. Place potatoes on a cookie sheet and allow to cool. After cooling, peel all pieces and cut up into ½-inch pieces.

Start eggs in cold water and boil for at least 12 minutes. Empty hot water off eggs and place in cold water and ice cubes until eggs are completely cold. Peel and mash eggs over potatoes in a bowl.

Add pickle relish, onion powder, celery seed and garlic powder to taste. Mix in mayonnaise and mustard completely and store in the refrigerator overnight before serving.

Joanne Narramore
Susanville, California • Lassen Municipal Utility District

Panzanella Salad

About 12 to 15 tomatoes
Salt, to taste
1 to 2 bunches green onions, finely chopped
1 to 2 jalapeno peppers, sliced around seeds and chopped
Big bunch of basil, cut or torn into ribbons (don't do this until you are ready to assemble)
1 loaf hard bread
Olive oil

The night before, tear up a loaf of bread into large croutons. Let sit on the counter all night to dry out. In the morning, heat the oven to 375 degrees. Put croutons on a jelly pan and toast in the oven for 15 to 20 minutes, until crisp. You may choose to toss them in olive oil before toasting.

If you choose, you can forget the night-before business and just toast the croutons in the oven.

Slice the tomatoes in very fine, thin wedges. Place tomatoes in a colander in the sink and sprinkle with salt, to taste. Let the tomatoes sit and drain for about an hour. The seeds will disappear as will lots of the juice.

When drained, mix onions and jalapenos with tomatoes.

Assemble in a large bowl: half croutons, half tomato mixture, half basil. Repeat.

Drizzle with olive oil. Garnish with a few croutons and basil leaves. It's OK to let it sit at room temperature about 1 to 2 hours. Toss when ready to serve.

Christi Clark
Neskowin, Oregon • Tillamook PUD

Pineapple Pecan Chicken Salad

6 to 8 chicken breasts
2 c. mayonnaise
1 Tbsp. onion powder
2 Tbsp. fresh parsley, chopped
¼ c. bell pepper, chopped
1 tsp. white pepper
¼ c. sugar
3 c. celery, diced finely
15-oz. can crushed pineapple, drain and reserve juice
16-oz. can water chestnuts, chopped
1 c. pecan pieces
Salt and pepper, to taste

Cook chicken breasts in boiling salted water with celery leaves. When done, drain chicken from water, then cool, dice and chop.

In a large bowl, combine mayonnaise, onion powder, parsley, pepper and sugar. Blend until smooth. Fold in drained pineapple, celery, water chestnuts, chicken and pecans. Mixture should be moist, but not too wet. If too dry, add pineapple juice, one tablespoon at a time, until desired consistency. Add salt and pepper, to taste.

Serve on leaf lettuce or bread.

Pepper Wendt
Bagdad, Florida • Escambia River Electric Cooperative

Pineapple Salad

20-oz. can pineapple chunks or tidbits, reserve juice
Juice from 1 orange
Juice from 1 lemon
1 c. sugar
1 egg, beaten well
3 Tbsp. cornstarch
1 c. whipping cream
2 tsp. sugar
1 tsp. vanilla
Bananas, sliced
Maraschino cherries (optional)
Nuts (optional)

Combine juices, 1 c. sugar and egg in a saucepan. Mix a small amount of juice with the cornstarch. Add to the juice mixture and cook until thick, stirring constantly to prevent scorching. Chill thoroughly.

Stiffly whip cream with 2 tsp. sugar and vanilla. Fold into juice mixture.

Layer dressing, sliced bananas (as many as you want) and pineapple chunks or tidbits. Repeat layers, ending with the dressing.

Garnish with maraschino cherries and nuts.

Our family always had this salad at Christmas and Thanksgiving. I got the recipe from my Auntie Ruby in 1957. Mom told me that Auntie Ruby got the recipe in about 1928 from high school.

Linda Fitzgerald
Tillamook, Oregon • Tillamook PUD

Pink Cranberry Salad

1 c. sugar
1 lb. fresh cranberries, chopped (or frozen cranberries chopped while still frozen)
1 lb. small marshmallows
1 large can crushed pineapple, including juice
2 c. heavy whipping cream

Mix together the sugar, cranberries, marshmallows and pineapple and chill overnight. The next day, whip the cream. Mix with the chilled ingredients. Store in the refrigerator.

This salad is the one recipe that all my children use at their family celebrations.

Anne Hanson
Bend, Oregon • Central Oregon Electric Cooperative

Pink Salad

8½-oz. can crushed pineapple
6-oz. package raspberry Jell-O
8 oz. cream cheese, beaten until soft
1 can whole cranberry sauce
½ to 1 c. walnuts, chopped
1 c. Cool Whip

Drain pineapple, then add water to measure 2 c. Heat liquid to boiling. Dissolve Jell-O in the hot liquid, and chill to soft stage.

Add cream cheese, cranberry sauce, walnuts and Cool Whip. Top with extra Cool Whip.

Thirty-five-plus years ago a friend shared this recipe. Dot Patterson is now with her Lord, but we can't forget her because our holiday dinners wouldn't be as great without her cranberry salad. My grandkids changed the name to Pink Salad.

Adeline Knorr
The Dalles, Oregon • Northern Wasco County PUD

Potato Salad

12 c. potatoes, cooked and shredded
1 c. celery, chopped
1 c. onion, chopped
12 hard-boiled eggs, diced
3 c. salad dressing
4 tsp. salt
6 Tbsp. mustard
2 c. sugar
¼ c. vinegar
½ c. milk

Toss together in a large bowl.

Mrs. Marcus Plank
Alturas, California • Surprise Valley Electrification

Pretzel Salad

Pretzel layer:

2½ c. small pretzels, broken

½ c. butter or margarine (not low fat)

2 Tbsp. sugar

In a frying pan over medium heat, melt butter. Stir in sugar then add pretzels. Stir and heat several minutes, until most butter is absorbed. Place in a 9-by-13-inch pan or ovenproof casserole dish. Bake for 10 minutes in 350-degree oven. Cool.

Cream layer:

8 oz. cream cheese, at room temperature

1 c. powdered sugar

8 oz. Cool Whip, thawed

In a medium bowl, beat cream cheese until smooth. Beat in powdered sugar. Fold in Cool Whip. Spread evenly over cooled pretzels.

Jell-O layer:

6 oz. strawberry Jell-O

2½ c. boiling water

2 10-oz. packages frozen strawberries (see note below)

Dissolve Jell-O in hot water. Stir in strawberries, and set in a cool place to thicken. When soft-set, spread over cream cheese mixture.

Note: Make Jell-O first and allow it to set while the rest of dish is prepared. Do not allow Jell-O to become firm.

I use berries from my home freezer. Measure berries and water separately to total 40 ounces.

Frozen raspberries and raspberry Jell-O can be used, or try lime Jell-O with pineapple and mandarin oranges.

Wini Whitaker
Redmond, Oregon • Central Electric Cooperative

Red, White and Black Bean Salad

15-oz. can cannellini beans, rinsed and drained

15-oz. can black beans, rinsed and drained

3 Roma tomatoes, cut into chunks

1 red pepper, chopped

½ c. salsa

4 green onions, diced

¼ c. red wine vinegar

2 Tbsp. fresh cilantro, chopped

Salt and pepper, to taste

Combine all vegetables and cilantro in a large bowl. Mix salsa, red wine vinegar, salt and pepper, and pour over vegetables. Toss.

Pepper Wendt
Bagdad, Florida • Escambia River Electric Cooperative

Russian Beet Salad 'Stolichniy'

3 medium potatoes

3 medium carrots

3 medium beets

1 onion, cubed

3 dill pickles, cubed

1 green apple, cubed

1 can peas

3 Tbsp. mayonnaise

Small bunch parsley

Small bunch dill

Salt and pepper, to taste

Lemon salt, to taste

Strips of red pepper and black olives for decoration

Wash potatoes, carrots and beets; place in a pot. Add cold water to cover. Bring to a boil. Reduce heat and cook for 25 to 30 minutes. Drain the water and let the veggies cool.

Peel the potatoes, carrots and beets, then cube. Mix well with apple, pickles and onion. Add parsley, dill, salt, pepper and lemon salt. Add mayonnaise and peas.

Place on a large plate and decorate with red pepper and black olives.

Larissa Phillips
Pahrump, Nevada • Valley Electric Association

Super Coldslaw

1 tsp. salt

¼ tsp. pepper

½ tsp. dry mustard

2 Tbsp. sugar

1½ Tbsp. yellow or sweet onion, grated

3 Tbsp. salad oil or extra virgin olive oil

⅓ c. apple cider vinegar

3 c. cabbage mix

¼ c. green pepper

3 Tbsp. pimento

Mix the first seven ingredients to create the sauce.

In a medium-size glass bowl, mix chopped cabbage, green pepper and pimento. Add the mixed sauce and thoroughly incorporate.

Cover the bowl and refrigerate for about half an hour. Stir it once more and cover.

Serve with your favorite entrée. Try it in fish tacos or serve as a side with Mexican dishes. Excellent at picnics.

This recipe is a family and friends' favorite as it is tasty and versatile.

Christine Sundquist
Camp Sherman, Oregon • Central Electric Cooperative

Thai Beef Salad

12 oz. double carrot lettuce blend
16 oz. tri-color deli coleslaw blend
3 stalks celery, trimmed and sliced
2 Tbsp. chives, snipped
¼ c. basil, snipped
1½ lbs. ground beef
½ c. gourmet sauce (Yoshida's or Asian brand)
⅓ c. extra-crunchy peanut butter
⅓ c. coconut, toasted
20-oz. can crushed pineapple, drained
½ c. mayonnaise
½ c. sour cream
¼ c. granulated sugar
1½ tsp. lemon juice
1½ c. crunchy chow mein noodles or wonton strips

Preheat oven to 425 degrees. Line a baking sheet with parchment paper or baking mat. Toast coconut for 3 to 4 minutes, or until light golden brown.

In a large skillet over medium heat, brown ground beef until it is no longer pink, and drain off fat. Whisk together gourmet sauce and peanut butter and stir into cooked ground beef. Simmer for 2 minutes. Remove from heat and set aside to cool completely.

In a large serving bowl, toss together double carrot lettuce blend, tri-color deli coleslaw blend, celery, chives and basil. Garnish salad mixture with seasoned ground beef, toasted coconut and chow mein noodles.

In a small mixing bowl, whisk together mayonnaise, sour cream, sugar and lemon juice. Stir in crushed pineapple.

Serve salad with pineapple dressing.

Shelly Bevington
Hermiston, Oregon • Umatilla Electric

Tortellini Salad

4 9-oz. packages cheese-filled tortellini
14-oz. can artichoke bottoms, drained and chopped; reserve liquid
15-oz. jar roasted red peppers, drained and chopped
12-oz. package dry salami, cubed
2 medium zucchini, cubed
1 medium purple onion, diced

Cook tortellini per package directions. Rinse, drain and cool. Add all ingredients in a large bowl. Mix well and set aside.

Dressing:

¼ c. balsamic vinegar
¼ c. fresh basil, finely chopped
1 tsp. salt
¼ tsp. fresh coarse-ground black pepper
2 cloves garlic, minced
Reserved liquid from artichoke hearts

Combine all ingredients in a bowl and whisk together until well blended. Pour over salad, chill and serve.

Claudia Milazzo
Brookings, Oregon • Coos-Curry Electric Cooperative

Soups

Baked Potato Cheesy Soup

⅔ c. butter
⅔ c. flour
7 c. milk
4 large baking potatoes, baked, peeled and cubed (about 4 c.)
4 green onions, sliced thinly
12 bacon strips, cooked, drained and crumbled
1¼ c. mild Cheddar cheese, shredded
1 c. sour cream
¾ tsp. salt
½ tsp. pepper

In a large Dutch oven or stockpot, melt butter over low heat. Stir in flour and continue to heat and stir until smooth.

Gradually add milk, stirring constantly until sauce has thickened. Add potatoes and onions. Bring to a boil, stirring constantly. Reduce heat and simmer for 10 minutes. Add remaining ingredients and stir until cheese is melted. Serve immediately.

In a hurry, I have boiled my potatoes and used bacon bits. Almost as good.

Frances Hodge
Milton, Florida • Escambia River Electric Cooperative

Bay Scallop Chowder

3 medium potatoes, diced
1 small carrot, chopped
1 stalk celery, chopped
1 medium onion, chopped
2 c. chicken stock
½ tsp. salt
¼ tsp. freshly ground pepper
½ bay leaf
½ tsp. thyme, crumbled
1 pound fresh bay scallops
1 pound fresh mushrooms, sliced
1½ Tbsp. butter
½ c. dry white wine
1 c. heavy cream
1 egg yolk, lightly beaten
2 Tbsp. parsley, chopped
Paprika

Place potatoes, carrots, celery and onion in a large pot. Cover with chicken stock and bring to a boil. Add salt, pepper, bay leaf and thyme. Simmer, covered, until vegetables are tender.

Remove bay leaf and transfer mixture to blender or food processor. Blend until smooth.

Meanwhile, sauté mushrooms in butter. Add scallops and wine and cook for 1 minute. Stir in cream mixed with egg yolk. Combine this mixture with the puréed vegetables and broth. Heat through and serve with a sprinkling of parsley and paprika.

This was our special-occasion soup when we lived in Alaska.

Jan Haugh
Challis, Idaho • Salmon River Electric Cooperative

Brad's Corn Chowder

1 qt. half-and-half, divided
4 ears corn, white or yellow
6 slices thick bacon, cut crosswise into small pieces
1 medium yellow onion, diced
1 medium potato, diced
4 to 6 garlic cloves, minced
Salt and pepper, to taste

Cut the corn kernels from the cobs. Set kernels aside. Cut onions and potatoes into corn kernel-sized chunks.

Cut the corn cobs in half, if needed, and add to a large pot. Add just enough half-and-half to cover. Bring to a low simmer for 10 minutes. Do not boil.

While the cobs simmer, cook the bacon in a medium pan over medium-high heat. When just starting to crisp, remove excess fat but leave about 2 Tbsp. Add potatoes and sauté until partially cooked, then add the onion and garlic. Cook until potatoes and onion are tender. Season to taste with salt and pepper.

Remove the cobs and discard them. Transfer the potato and onion mixture to the half-and-half. Add the corn kernels and simmer uncovered for 15 minutes (do not allow to boil). Just before done, add more half-and-half (or maybe a little heavy cream) for desired consistency. Heat and serve.

Do not cut corn from cob by standing on end. This is dangerous and messy. Try this: Lay the cob on a cutting board and cut along one side from end to end, slicing off two or three rows of corn at a time. Roll the cob a little and repeat. It only takes about 6 slices to complete the job with no mess.

James B. Pearson
Bandon, Oregon • Coos-Curry Electric Cooperative

Chili

1 lb. ground buffalo (or ground beef)
½ c. chopped onion
¾ c. water
½ c. chopped green pepper
2 to 3 tsp. chili powder
½ tsp. salt
¼ tsp. hot pepper sauce
2 cloves of garlic, minced
28-oz. can diced tomatoes, drained
1 can tomato soup
6-oz. can tomato paste
4-oz. can green chilies
15-oz. can black beans, drained
15-oz. can dark red kidney beans, drained
Shredded cheese (optional)

Brown meat, onion and garlic together. Mix the rest of the ingredients in a large pot and add meat mixture. Bring to a boil; cover and simmer for at least an hour. Top with onions and shredded cheese, if desired.

Our favorite recipe when winter comes.

Kris Barker
Eugene, Oregon • Lane Electric Cooperative

Christi's Tortilla Soup

Soup base:
Oil
Onion, diced
Garlic, chopped
Package of chicken, bones and skin OK
32-oz. nonfat chicken broth
Jalapeno pepper, chopped
8-oz. can corn
16-oz. can diced tomatoes
8 oz. beans (optional)
2 or 3 yellow squash, peeled and diced

Sauté onions and garlic in oil; remove from pan. Sauté chicken. Add broth, onions and garlic; simmer until chicken falls off the bone. Remove chicken from the pan; debone and remove skin. Add chicken, corn, tomatoes and beans to broth. About five minutes before serving, add squash. The base can be made a day or two ahead of serving.

Salsa:
Tomatoes, diced
Rock salt
Jalapeno pepper, diced
Cucumber, cored (to remove seeds) and diced
3 or 4 green onions, chopped
Cilantro, chopped

Dice tomatoes and put in a colander sitting on a plate. Sprinkle salt over tomatoes. Let it sit about 30 minutes; it will drain away some of the liquid and the seeds. Add remaining ingredients and let marinate about 1 hour before serving.

Garnishes:
Salsa
Avocado, cut into big chunks
Mexican white cheese, crumbled
4 or 5 tortillas, cut up into ribbons and fried in hot oil
Cilantro, chopped

Christi Clark
Neskowin, Oregon • Tillamook PUD

Corn and Crab Bisque

2 sticks butter
1 large yellow onion, chopped
2 Tbsp. garlic, chopped
1 can creamed corn
1 can whole-kernel corn
1 c. flour
3 c. chicken stock
1 qt. heavy cream
½ lb. lump crabmeat
1 bunch green onion, chopped
Salt and pepper, to taste
Old Bay Seasoning (optional)
Large chunks of fish (optional)

Melt the butter in a heavy-bottom pot. Sauté the chopped onions, garlic and both cans of corn for 5 minutes.

Stir in the flour until all is incorporated. Slowly blend in the chicken stock, stirring continuously.

Bring this mixture to a slow boil for 15 minutes. At this point, you may add, if desired, large chunks of fish (I use flounder).

Cook for 10 minutes longer. Add the heavy cream and season to taste with salt and black pepper. Finish with green onions and crabmeat.

Jean Wendt
Milton, Florida

Creamy Clam Chowder

1 large onion, chopped
3 medium carrots, chopped
2 celery ribs, sliced
¾ c. butter, cubed
2 10¾-oz. cans condensed cream of potato soup, undiluted
3 6½-oz. cans minced clams
2 Tbsp. cornstarch
1 qt. half-and-half

In a large saucepan, sauté the onion, carrots and celery in butter until tender. Stir in the potato soup and two cans of undrained clams. Drain and discard the juice from the remaining can of clams. Add the clams to the soup.

Combine cornstarch and a small amount of half-and-half until smooth, and stir into soup. Add the remaining half-and-half. Bring to a boil. Cook and stir for 2 minutes, or until thickened.

Mary Walker
Ione, Oregon • Columbia Basin Electric Cooperative

Dan's Oregon Chili

1 lb. ground venison or elk meat
1 303-size can red beans
1 303-size can stewed tomatoes
6 red or white radishes, diced
½ tsp. salt
2 tsp. chili powder
½ Tbsp. garlic salt
1 Tbsp. honey
1 small onion, diced
8-oz. can tomato sauce
1 can water
Cheese, grated

Fry meat, onion and radishes together. Add 1 tsp. oil and cook until browned. Add other ingredients, except cheese, and bring to a boil.

Simmer about an hour. Stir often. Add honey last; it tends to stick. Add cheese, to taste.

My husband invented this recipe for a cooking contest November 11, 2004. He was voted first-prize winner by the judges and hospital board. We really enjoy it at home and so do our friends.

Lynn Thies
Brookings, Oregon • Coos-Curry Electric Cooperative

Gazpacho

3 c. fresh tomatoes, peeled and chopped
½ c. green pepper, chopped
½ c. onion, chopped
¼ c. fresh parsley
2 c. cucumbers, seeded and chopped
2½ tsp. salt
1 clove garlic, crushed
⅓ c. olive oil (scant)
3 Tbsp. fresh lemon juice
3 Tbsp. red wine vinegar
2 c. tomato juice
1 tsp. hot pepper sauce
1 Tbsp. Worcestershire sauce

Put all vegetables in a food processor and pulse until well chopped. Add remaining ingredients. Chill well. Serve with a dollop of sour cream or garnish with a fresh, peeled shrimp.

Carole Royer
River Ranch, Florida • Peace River Electric Cooperative

The Great Russian Borsch Recipe

2 lbs. neck or shoulder pork meat on bones
2 big beets
½ medium green cabbage
2 medium carrots
1 onion
3 potatoes
1 Tbsp. tomato paste
2 Tbsp. olive oil
1 Tbsp. brown sugar
1 Tbsp. lemon juice
3 cloves garlic
1 small bunch parsley
1 small bunch dill
2 strips bacon
Sour cream
Salt
Black pepper
Lemon salt

Wash meat. Place in a big pot and fill with 12 c. cold water. Bring to a boil and clear the foam. Add 1 whole carrot and 1 whole onion for the broth to be clear and transparent. Reduce the heat and cook meat over medium heat for about 50 minutes.

While meat is cooking, shred the cabbage finely and place in a bowl.

Place a frying pan on medium heat. Add olive oil and chopped onions. Cook until golden brown. Add cubed carrots and cook for about 5 minutes.

Wash, peel and cube the beets. Add to a frying pan and cook for 5 to 8 minutes. Add brown sugar, lemon juice and tomato paste. Mix it well and cook on low heat for about 15 minutes.

After cooking meat for 50 minutes, add shredded green cabbage. Cook on medium heat for 20 minutes. Add peeled and cubed potatoes, then add veggies from frying pan. Cook for 25 to 30 minutes on low heat.

Finely chop garlic cloves, parsley, dill and bacon and add to pot. At the same time, add salt, pepper and lemon salt, to taste. Simmer for 10 to 15 minutes.

Serve with 1 Tbsp. sour cream per bowl and garnish with fresh herbs.

All my friends love borsch and salads that I make.

Larissa Phillips
Pahrump, Nevada • Valley Electric Association

Mintmier's Chicken Tortilla Soup

6 Tbsp. vegetable oil
1 Tbsp. chili powder
8 corn tortillas, chopped
3 bay leaves
8 cloves garlic, minced
6 c. chicken broth
½ c. fresh cilantro, chopped
1 tsp. salt
1 onion, chopped
½ tsp. cayenne pepper
29-oz. can diced tomatoes
5 boneless chicken breast halves, cooked
1 c. picante sauce
2 Tbsp. ground cumin

Cook chicken in a pot of water for 20 minutes. In a large pot, heat oil. Add tortillas, garlic, cilantro and onion. Sauté for a few minutes. Stir in tomatoes and picante sauce. Bring to a boil. Add cumin, chili powder, bay leaves and chicken broth. Return to a boil. Reduce heat to medium. Add salt and cayenne pepper.

Simmer for 30 minutes, uncovered. Remove bay leaves and add chicken. Heat through and serve. Great with chips, guacamole, cheese or sour cream.

Tina Mintmier
Clio, California • Plumas-Sierra Rural Electric Cooperative

Patsy's She Crab Soup

1 stick butter
½ c. flour
1 c. onions and celery, finely chopped
1 pt. chicken broth
2 qt. half-and-half
½ bottle Chef Paul Prudhomme's blackened redfish seasoning
1 Tbsp. Louisiana hot sauce
1 Tbsp. white or black pepper
1 lb. lump crabmeat
1 lb. small shrimp, peeled and deveined
3 green onions, chopped

Melt butter in a Dutch oven. Add onions and celery. Sauté until almost tender. Add flour and brown as a roux. Add all seasonings. As the soup thickens, add chicken broth and, stirring as not to stick. Add shrimp and cook until light pink. Add crabmeat and half-and-half. Cook on low heat, 5 to 8 minutes, stirring as not to stick. Add green onions and cook 5 minutes.

Serve in bread bowl with croutons.

Elizabeth (Patsy) Miller
Southport, Florida • Gulf Coast Electric Cooperative

Potato Dumpling Soup

1 Tbsp. chicken-flavored base
1 carrot, shredded
4 medium-sized potatoes, cubed
1 small onion, finely chopped (about ½ c.)
2 eggs
2 c. flour
2 c. half-and-half
1 c. milk
1 Tbsp. dry parsley
Salt and pepper, to taste
Cheddar cheese, shredded (optional)

Put vegetables in a big soup kettle. Cover vegetables with water (almost half of the kettle) and bring to a boil.

While vegetables are cooking, mix eggs, flour and water to make a soft dough. Drop dough by ½ Tbsp. into boiling water and cook for 5 to 10 minutes.

Add half-and-half, milk, parsley, salt and pepper. Bring to a boil again, then simmer to thicken. Add Cheddar cheese on top.

Annette Kubishta
Pendleton, Oregon

Savory Stew

1½ to 2 lbs. beef stew meat, cut into pieces
2 c. unpeeled red potatoes, cut into chunks
2 c. carrots, cut into chunks
2 c. celery, cut into chunks
1 onion, cut into chunks
1 Tbsp. sugar
1 Tbsp. flour
1 can tomato soup
½ soup can red wine (or water)
Garlic salt, to taste
Pepper, to taste
Italian seasoning, to taste

Place meat and vegetables in a Dutch oven or large casserole. Season with garlic salt, pepper and Italian seasoning. Add sugar, flour, soup and wine or water. Mix together, cover, and bake at 250 degrees for 5 to 5½ hours. Keep the lid on and do not disturb until it's done.

This recipe has been in our family since 1948.

Rosemary Soper
Bellevue, Washington, and Manzanita, Oregon • Tillamook PUD

Southwestern Chili and Ale

1 lb. ground beef, crumbled
1 lb. ground pork, crumbled
1 large sweet onion, peeled and diced
1 large green pepper, trimmed, seeded and diced
2 tsp. salt, divided
4 Tbsp. chili powder mix (I use Mojave brand with
    chili pepper, cumin, oregano, salt and garlic)
1 tsp. ground coriander
½ tsp. ground black pepper
2 c. fresh tomatoes diced (may use canned
    in juice, but omit 1 tsp. salt)
1¾ c. water
½ c. masa harina flour (may use all-purpose flour)
2 15-oz. cans chili beans with sauce
12 oz. white ale (I use Blue Moon with coriander and orange peel)
2 Tbsp. each lemon and lime juice (may use ¼ c. lime juice)
Mexican blend shredded cheese
Sour cream
Fresh cilantro, chopped

Spray slow-cooker insert with nonstick cooking spray and turn
to low heat setting. In the insert, toss together crumbled ground
beef, crumbled ground pork, onion, green pepper and 1 tsp.
salt. Place on lid and cook on low heat for 3½ hours, or until
meat is no longer pink. Drain off excess fat.

In a small mixing bowl, combine tomatoes with 1 tsp. salt.
Season meat mixture with chili powder mix, ground coriander and black pepper. Let spices cook for 5 minutes to release
flavor. Stir in tomatoes, whisked-together water and flour, chili
beans with sauce, white ale and citrus juices.

Place on lid and cook on low heat for 1½ hours, or until
heated through and ready to serve. Serve garnished with cheese,
sour cream and cilantro.

While trying to find ways to use up garden tomatoes this past season, I decided to try out a Southwestern spin on a restaurant recipe beer chili from a cookbook I have. It was the best chili I have ever made.

Shelly Bevington
Hermiston, Oregon • Umatilla Electric

Squash or Pumpkin Soup

3 Tbsp. butter
1 clove garlic
1 onion, chopped
2 c. baked or steamed pumpkin or squash
Broth or milk
Salt and pepper, to taste
Parmesan cheese

In a medium fry pan, melt the butter. Add the clove of garlic
and onion and fry until tender. Add the pumpkin or squash
and stir together. Add enough milk or broth to make desired
consistency, and salt and pepper.

Simmer until everything is well cooked. Strain the mixture
through a colander or blend in a blender. If desired, more milk
or broth may be added. Serve with Parmesan cheese on top.

Kay Antunez de Mayolo
Eagleville, California • Surprise Valley Electrification

Taco Soup

1 lb. lean ground beef
3 Tbsp. taco seasoning mix
1 can chili with beans or 2 c. homemade chili
½ large onion or 3 to 4 green onions
1 Tbsp. tomato paste
1 c. frozen corn or 1 can of corn
1 corn tortilla, cut in half and then into strips
3 c. chicken broth
1 c. Cheddar cheese, grated
2 c. tortilla chips, crushed

Brown beef over medium-high heat in a Dutch oven. Drain fat.
Add taco seasoning and stir well for 1 minute, then add chili,
onion, tomato paste and tortilla strips and bring to a boil, stirring well. Add chicken broth and bring back to a boil, stirring
well.

Simmer for 10 to 15 minutes, stirring occasionally. Serve in
large soup bowls topped with cheese and tortilla chips.

Alan Ciszeski

Taco Soup

2 lbs. hamburger
1 large onion, chopped
4 oz. to 8 oz. mild green chilies, chopped
1 heaping Tbsp. minced garlic
2 tsp. chili powder
½ tsp. cumin

1 tsp. salt
Pinch of pepper
½ c. salsa
1 qt. pinto beans
14-oz. can kidney beans
1 qt. canned or frozen chopped tomatoes
8-oz. can tomato sauce
3 c. corn, canned or frozen
1 large can black olives, pitted and sliced
2 c. to 4 c. beef broth

Toppings:
Tortilla chips
Cheese, grated
Sour cream

Brown meat and add onion, garlic, chilies and spices. Add the rest of the ingredients and simmer. The longer the better; I do mine for half a day. If using canned foods, add the juices, too.

Serve topped with tortilla chips, cheese and sour cream.

A fall or winter favorite of our family.

Valerie Giesbrecht
Othello, Washington • Big Bend Electric Cooperative

Taco Soup

1 lb. ground chuck
1 package taco seasoning
15-oz. can pinto beans, rinsed and drained
1 c. whole-kernel corn
15-oz. can tomatoes, diced with peppers and onions
2 c. water
1 Tbsp. sugar

Coat a skillet with nonstick spray. Cook ground chuck until done, stirring frequently. Add remaining ingredients. Reduce heat and simmer for 15 minutes.

I always add more peppers and onions to the ground chuck.

Shirley Glessmer
Wauchula, Florida • Peace River Electric Cooperative

Tom's Oxtail Stew

3 packages oxtails
1½ c. flour
2 tsp. garlic powder
2 tsp. salt
2 tsp. pepper
½ c. oil
2 large potatoes
4 stalks celery
2 large onions
4 carrots
3 bay leaves
1 large can diced tomatoes
2 tsp. paprika

Season flour with paprika, salt, pepper and garlic powder.

Coat the meat with the seasoned flour; brown on all sides in a fry pan.

Place the meat in 3-qt. casserole dish and add carrots, onions, celery, potatoes and tomatoes. Add liquid from the frying pan until the liquid reaches 1 inch from the top cover.

Place the bay leaves on top. Cover and bake at 325 degrees for 3 to 4 hours, until meat is tender.

Thomas S. Koskey
Pahrump, Nevada • Valley Electric Association

Yummy Chicken Tortilla Soup

4 onions, chopped
6 large tomatoes, diced, or 2 28-oz. cans diced tomatoes
1 tsp. olive oil
3 tsp. dried oregano
¾ tsp. ground cumin
4 Tbsp. garlic cloves, minced
6 c. chicken broth
½ tsp. salt
6 corn tortillas, cut into ¼-inch strips
3 chicken breasts, boiled and shredded
½ c. mozzarella cheese, shredded
6 lime wedges (optional)
Avocado, cubed (optional)
Cilantro, chopped (optional)
Low-fat sour cream or plain Greek yogurt (optional)

Preheat oven to 350 degrees. Place strips of tortillas in a single layer on a baking sheet. Bake for 12 minutes, or until toasted.

Combine onions and tomatoes in a blender until smooth.

Heat oil on medium high in a big pot. Add oregano, cumin and minced garlic; sauté for 10 seconds. Add puréed onion mixture to pot and cook for 1 minute on high. Stir in chicken broth and salt. Bring to a boil. Reduce heat and simmer for 15 minutes.

Ladle soup into bowls and top with the baked tortilla strips, shredded chicken and cheese. Serve with optional lime wedges, avocado, cilantro, and sour cream or yogurt.

Amy Hackbarth
Bend, Oregon • Central Electric Cooperative

Variety

Homemade Noodles

1 c. flour
½ tsp. salt
2 tsp. baking powder
½ c. butter, softened
2 eggs
⅛ c. milk

Mix dry ingredients in a bowl, then cream butter into dry ingredients. In a small bowl, mix eggs and milk. Add to the dry ingredients and butter.

Roll on to the counter, thin like noodles you buy. Cover with a towel and let dry all day. Add to your chicken soup.

Glenda Gheen
Redmond, Oregon • Central Electric Cooperative

Fig Vinaigrette

1 c. rice vinegar
½ c. figs, chopped
1 Tbsp. sugar

Soak overnight and then put all in a food processor. It is wonderful as a salad dressing.

If you don't like it so thick, remove some of the figs.

Teri Hruska
Fairbanks, Alaska • Golden Valley Electric Association

Joe's Five-Star Seafood Boil

¼ c. onion, chopped
¼ c. celery, chopped
3 to 4 garlic cloves, minced
1 tsp. parsley flakes or sprigs
⅛ c. bell pepper, chopped
2 c. water
Salt and pepper, to taste

Bring all ingredients to a boil for 3 minutes. Cover any type of shellfish in the water mixture and cook 3 to 5 minutes until done.

Use this seafood boil to steam oysters, clams or mussels. Lobsters can be steamed or boiled in a double batch.

A roux can be made of remaining liquid with brown rice flour, regular flour or cornstarch mixture for a dipping sauce, or spread on angel hair pasta. Add salt and pepper to roux, to taste.

Joseph Champion
Westwood, California • Lassen Municipal Utility District

Lime and Lemonade

½ c. fresh lime juice
½ c. fresh lemon juice
¾ c. sugar
4 c. cold water
½ lemon, sliced
½ lime, sliced

In a pitcher, combine juices and sugar. Stir to dissolve the sugar. Add the remaining ingredients and stir until well blended.

This is a very refreshing easy drink on a hot summer day. I have used the bottled juice from the store when I didn't have fresh limes and lemons.

Candace Zaugg
Tillamook, Oregon • Tillamook PUD

Meat Marinade

2 tsp. oil
¼ c. soy sauce
1 tsp. garlic powder
1½ tsp. vinegar
1 tsp. pepper
3 Tbsp. sesame seeds
⅛ tsp. cayenne
2 green onions

Toast the sesame seeds in a frying pan until brown, then crush them with a rolling pin.

Add all ingredients together, and marinate for two to three days.

This is great for deer, elk or beef steaks.

This is a favorite of all my family.

Glenda Gheen
Redmond, Oregon • Central Electric Cooperative

Mom's Original Spaghetti Sauce

5 large onions, diced or minced
3 green peppers, diced or minced
2 lbs. (1 can) tomatoes
3 small cans tomato paste
4 cloves garlic
1 lb. lean ground beef
½ lb. chopped pork
1 heaping tsp. celery seed
1 tsp. salt
½ tsp. red pepper (or to taste)

Brown beef and pork in olive oil. Add the other ingredients; simmer 1½ to 2 hours (water may be added). Garlic cloves will rise to the top; mash and leave in.

Dating from 1955, and 50-plus years later still the most often requested favorite.

Jane Streek
Alpharetta, Georgia • Klickitat PUD

Strip Strip Sauce

2 medium white onions
6 large saltwater-brined male herring
Melt from each male fish—each has 2 melt
8 large russett potatoes
Butter
3 heaping Tbsp. sour cream
1 c., or more if needed, heavy whipping
   cream; sauce should not be runny
Small amount of vinegar

Soak the brined herring in water for approximately 2 days in the refrigerator. Change the water three times a day; this removes the salt brine from the fish.

Take the male herring fish and cut the fins, tail and head off and scrape thoroughly to remove all of the scales. Cut the fish open and remove all of the contents inside the fish.

Save the melt and place in a separate bowl, and add a small amount of vinegar, less than a teaspoon, to the melt. Work the vinegar into the melt until you remove all of the scriffen that houses the melt. Throw the scriffen away. Add the heavy cream to the melt and beat with a fork until smooth; set aside.

Dice the onions and the herring. Place both in a bowl. Add the melt mixture, stir thoroughly and place in the refrigerator for 24 hours.

Boil the potatoes with the skins on until soft. Remove the skins and slice each potato lengthwise into 4 slices. Add butter.

Pour the melt sauce over the soft hot buttered potatoes.

Jacqueline Herrin
Salmon, Idaho • Salmon River Electric Cooperative

Vegetables

Carrot Soufflé

7 c. carrots (about 2 lbs.)
⅓ c. granulated sugar
¼ c. sour cream (regular, non-fat or low-fat)
3 Tbsp. all-purpose flour
2 Tbsp. butter, melted
1 tsp. baking powder
1 tsp. vanilla extract
¼ tsp. salt
3 large egg yolks
Cooking spray
1 tsp. powdered sugar

Preheat oven to 350 degrees. Cook carrots in boiling water for 15 to 20 minutes, or until tender; drain. Place carrots in a food processor and process until smooth. Add granulated sugar and next seven ingredients. Pulse to combine.

Spoon mixture into a 2-qt. baking dish coated with cooking spray. Bake at 350 degrees for 40 minutes, or until puffed and set. Sprinkle with powdered sugar when cool.

This dish does not contain egg whites; therefore, it is not a true soufflé, yet the texture is light and fluffy.

Nora Simmons
Fairbanks, Alaska • Golden Valley Electric Association

Cheesy Scrumptious Potatoes

6 medium potatoes
2 c. Cheddar cheese, shredded
¼ c. butter
1½ c. sour cream
⅓ c. green onion, chopped
1 tsp. salt
¼ tsp. pepper
2 Tbsp. butter
Paprika

Cook potatoes in skins; cool. Peel and shred coarsely.

In a saucepan over low heat, combine cheese and ¼ c. butter. Stir constantly until almost melted. Remove from heat and blend in sour cream, onion and seasonings. Fold in potatoes and turn into greased 2-qt. casserole. Dot with 2 Tbsp. butter and sprinkle with paprika.

Bake, uncovered, in a 350-degree oven for 30 minutes, or until heated through.

If freezing, do so before baking and then allow to come to room temperature before baking.

This is a family favorite. It is usually always at a family gathering because someone always requests it.

Leanne Hockman
Bend, Oregon • Central Electric Cooperative

Country Corn Casserole

1 box cornbread mix
1 egg
1 can creamed corn
1 can regular corn (if you drain the corn,
    add 2 Tbsp. milk or cream)
1 onion, sliced
½ cube butter
Sour cream
Sliced chives, optional

Sauté sliced onions and butter until onions are tender. Mix cornbread mix, cans of corn and egg until smooth. Pour mixture into a 9-by-13-inch pan that has been greased with butter. Spread onions and butter on top. Add dollops of sour cream to the top. Sprinkle with chives.

Bake at 375 degrees for 40 minutes, or until golden brown.

Barbara Darland
Redmond, Oregon • Central Electric Cooperative

Dairy Potato Bake

2-lb. bag frozen hash brown potatoes, thawed
¾ c. melted butter, divided
1 tsp. salt
Dash of pepper
½ c. onion, chopped
10.5-oz. can cream chicken soup
12-oz. carton of sour cream
2 c. Cheddar cheese, grated
2 c. corn flakes, crushed
Paprika

In a large mixing bowl, stir together potatoes, ½ c. melted butter, salt, pepper, onion, soup, sour cream and cheese. Pour mixture into buttered 9-by-13-inch pan. Top with corn flake crumbs, drizzle with ¼ c. melted butter and sprinkle with paprika for added color.

Bake at 350 degrees for one hour.

Carla Smith
Benton City, Washington • Benton REA

Eggplant Parmesan

1 to 2 eggplant
2 eggs, scrambled
Flour
Italian bread crumbs
Salt
Pepper
26 oz. spaghetti sauce
1 lb. mozzarella cheese, cut into 16 slices
Parmesan cheese, shredded

Trim ends and slice eggplant into 16 half-inch slices. Shake in a bag with flour, salt and pepper. Dip in eggs, then a bowl of Italian bread crumbs. If you end up with more than 16 slices, go ahead and cook them, too.

Fry in a skillet with a little oil until browned. Flip and fry the other side. Drain on paper towels and set aside.

In a 9-by-13-inch baking dish, pour just enough spaghetti sauce to cover the bottom. Place eight slices of eggplant of mixed sizes in the baking dish, evenly spaced. Layer a slice of mozzarella on each and then 1 Tbsp. of spaghetti sauce. Don't fill the whole baking dish, just enough sauce to cover (not immerse) the slice of eggplant. Repeat with eggplant, cheese and sauce. If you have any sauce left over, distribute it on each stack. Top with grated Parmesan cheese.

Bake at 350 degrees for 20 to 30 minutes, until the cheese is melted and the sauce bubbly. Remove from oven and let stand for 10 minutes. You should end up with different-size eggplant stacks.

James B. Pearson
Bandon, Oregon • Coos-Curry Electric Cooperative

Eggplant Relish (Caponata)

½ c. olive oil, divided
1 large eggplant, peeled and diced
1 large onion, diced
6 stalks celery, diced
¼ c. fresh parsley, chopped
¼ c. fresh basil, chopped
Small can of diced tomatoes
½ c. red wine vinegar
6 tsp. sugar
About 6 green pitted olives, cut up
½ c. capers
½ c. pignoli nuts (optional)
Salt and pepper, to taste

Sauté onion and celery in ¼ c. olive oil. When done, remove from frying pan. Sauté eggplant in remaining oil. Add onion, celery, salt, pepper, parsley, basil and tomatoes. Mix vinegar and sugar and add to eggplant mixture.

Cook over low heat for 10 to 15 minutes, then add olives, capers and pignoli nuts. Cook for 10 minutes.

Cool and serve at room temperature or cold from the refrigerator.

Mae Gagliano
Staten Island, New York • Con Edison

Grandma's Baked Beans

2 cans northern beans
1 large can Bush's baked beans (any flavor)
Diced onions
½ c. brown sugar
Salt and pepper, to taste
Ham or bacon, diced
1 c. ketchup

Stir all together and add salt and pepper as needed. Bake at 350 degrees for one hour.

Denise Nielsen
Carnation, Washington

Green Stuffed Peppers

Green peppers
Cabbage
Salt
Sugar
White vinegar

Clean and cut the tops off the peppers. Save the tops. Let the pepper stand in salty water overnight, then rinse.

Shred cabbage and season with salt and sugar. Stuff peppers and sew on the tops or tie the tops on. Put peppers in a large jar (a gallon or larger). Pour white vinegar weakened with water over the peppers. Let them set. You do not have to seal the container. They will turn a lighter shade. Take one out and eat it.

Betty J. Phillips
West Richland, Washington • Benton REA

Jonathan's Baked Beans

1 lb. ground beef
½ c. brown sugar, packed
16-oz. can Campbell's baked beans (drained, if desired)
1 medium onion, chopped into small pieces
1 Tbsp. dry mustard

Brown beef and onions until translucent. Drain excess fat. Add sugar and mustard. Let simmer until sugar and mustard are blended well. Add beans. Place in an ovenproof casserole dish. Bake at 350 for 45 minutes.

This baked bean recipe has been the favorite of the family, especially our oldest son. He requested it so often we named it "Jonathan's Baked Beans."

Vera Holman
Las Vegas, Nevada

Martha's Montana Potatoes

5 lbs. potatoes
3 to 4 medium yellow onions
1 lb. bacon
Salt and pepper, to taste

Peel potatoes (or use white or red potatoes, which do not need to be peeled) and slice into half-inch slices. Slice onion.

Line bottom and sides of heavy cooking pot with bacon. Layer potatoes, onions, rest of bacon, salt and pepper alternately.

Cook on high for a few minutes until you can hear the bacon sizzling. Turn to simmer and continue cooking on stovetop for 1 to 2 hours. No need to stir.

Keri Taborski
Blairsden, California • Plumas-Sierra Rural Electric Cooperative

Mother's Stewed Okra

1½ lbs. okra, washed and okra, both ends
    trimmed off, sliced about ¼-inch thick
½ c. ham, diced
½ c. onion, diced
3 cloves garlic, diced
Oil
1 can chopped green chilies
16-oz. can crushed tomatoes
Salt and pepper, to taste

Sauté ham, onion and garlic in a small amount of oil, until onion is clear. Add okra, green chilies, crushed tomatoes, salt and pepper. Cook until tender.

Janet M. Cox
Thatcher, Arizona • Graham County Electric Cooperative

Party Carrots

1 to 1½ lbs. carrots, peeled and cooked
1 Tbsp. cornstarch
1 Tbsp. butter
1 tsp. lemon juice
¼ c. brown sugar
¼ c. white sugar
1 tsp. lemon or orange peel
½ c. fresh orange juice

Bring all ingredients (except for carrots) to a boil and cook until sauce is clear. Add carrots and allow to stand for 20 minutes. Is best made a day in advance of serving. Can substitute beets.

Carole Royer
River Ranch, Florida • Peace River Electric Cooperative

Party Potatoes

8 medium potatoes, peeled
1 tsp. salt
½ c. butter
4 oz. cream cheese
8 oz. sour cream
Paprika

Boil potatoes until tender and ready for mashing. Drain off all water. Mash potatoes with salt, butter, cream cheese and sour cream until smooth.

Put in a baking dish and bake at 350 degrees for 40 to 50 minutes, until lightly browned on top. Sprinkle a bit of paprika for color and serve.

These are served at every holiday meal in my family. We rarely have potatoes left over, so make plenty!

Marci Benoit
Coweta, Oklahoma • AEP (Public Service of Oklahoma)

Peony's Stuffed Pumpkin

1 c. cooked brown rice
1 stalk celery, chopped
¼ c. currants
¼ c. nuts—walnuts, pecans or chestnuts
1 Tbsp. fresh ginger, grated or finely chopped
1 medium pumpkin

Cut the top off the pumpkin and clean out the seeds. Oil the outer part of the pumpkin with your hands.

Heat a pan with oil. Sauté the celery until tender. Add the rice, currants, nuts and ginger (and other spices if you like). Toss well. Spoon the mixture into the pumpkin. Sit the cut lid on top.

Line a baking pan with parchment paper and sit the stuffed pumpkin on top. Bake at 350 degrees for 1 hour. After 1 hour, poke a knife into the bottom. If it goes in smoothly, it's done. Serve with or without gravy.

Peony Maeda and Sod Barkhas
Elmira, Oregon • Blachly-Lane Electric Cooperative

Pilgrim's (Maize/Corn) Pudding

2 Tbsp. cornstarch
¼ c. sugar
2 eggs, beaten slightly
2 Tbsp. butter, melted
14-oz. can cream-style corn
14-oz. can evaporated milk (non-fat or regular)
½ tsp. red-pepper flakes (optional)

Mix cornstarch and sugar. Add eggs and melted butter. Mix in the corn and evaporated milk.

Pour pudding into a greased 1-qt. casserole dish. Bake at 350 degrees for 45 minutes, or until it becomes like a soft-curd custard. Remove the dish from the oven and let it stand 5 minutes.

Sprinkle red-pepper flakes on top of pudding before baking. Serve hot or cold.

Deanna Bell
Sunriver, Oregon • Midstate Electric

Potatoes Au Gratin

30-oz. package shredded hash browns
16 oz. Cheddar cheese, shredded
1 tsp. salt
½ tsp. pepper
2 tsp. onion powder
1 pt. whipping cream
⅓ c. crushed buttery crackers
1 Tbsp. butter, melted

Grease a 9-by-13-inch glass baking dish. Arrange alternate layers of hash browns and shredded cheese. With each hash brown layer, sprinkle on salt, pepper and onion powder. Do as many layers as your dish allows—generally three layers—ending with cheese layer.

Pour whipping cream over the last cheese layer and top with crushed cracker crumbs. Drizzle melted butter over the top of the crumbs. Bake at 350 degrees for 45 minutes or until golden brown.

This can be made ahead and refrigerated or frozen.

This is a dish that is always requested by friends and family, whether it be a barbecue gathering or a holiday get-together.

Mary Walker
Ione, Oregon • Columbia Basin Electric Cooperative

Quick Stove-Top Scalloped Potatoes

6 medium-sized potatoes, peeled and sliced about ¼-inch thick
Salt and pepper, to taste
Garlic salt, to taste
¼ c. flour
Parsley flakes
Milk
½ c. cheese, grated
¼ cube margarine

Boil potatoes in enough water to cover the potatoes. Cook until tender; drain. Put in a frying pan and sprinkle with salt, pepper and garlic salt. Add ¼ c. flour and coat all potatoes and mix together. Sprinkle in a touch of parsley flakes. Add enough milk to cover potatoes, plus half above. Stir all together and let simmer until thick. Add grated cheese, plus pieces of margarine. Stir every once in a while.

Janet M. Cox
Thatcher, Arizona • Graham County Electric Cooperative

Rancho Beans

2 c. onion, chopped
1 lb. ground beef
1 c. ketchup
½ tsp. salt
1 Tbsp. mustard
2 16-oz. cans pork and beans
16-oz. can kidney beans
16-oz. can garbonzo beans

Brown onions and hamburger; drain. Add everything else and mix together. Put in a casserole dish. Bake for 30 minutes at 350 degrees.

Carrie Mace
Bend, Oregon • Central Electric Cooperative

Sweet Corn Casserole

6 Tbsp. unsalted butter, melted
2 tsp. salt
⅔ c. Parmesan cheese, freshly grated
1 tsp. sugar
1½ c. heavy cream
3 Tbsp. all-purpose flour
2 16-oz. bags frozen white corn, defrosted

Brush a 9-by-13-inch baking dish with some of the butter. Sprinkle ⅓ c. of the Parmesan over the bottom of the dish and tilt so the cheese is evenly distributed and adheres to the butter.

In a 4-quart saucepan, heat the cream until it begins to boil. Add the corn, salt and sugar. Heat, stirring occasionally, until the mixture is almost at a boil.

In the meantime, make a paste out of the remaining melted butter and flour. Stir into the mixture in the saucepan and cook until thickened and the liquid comes to a boil. Remove the pan from the heat. Transfer the mixture to the prepared dish and sprinkle with the remaining ⅓ c. cheese. At this point, you can let cool, cover and refrigerate for up to three days or freeze for up to one month. Bring to room temperature before continuing.

Preheat the oven to 350 degrees. Bake the corn dish until bubbling and golden brown, about 30 minutes.

Mary Ann Brolin
Blairsden, California • Plumas-Sierra Rural Electric Cooperative

Zucchini Patties

¼ c. oil
3 medium zucchini
½ red onion, diced
2 eggs, beaten
¼ c. parsley, chopped
½ c. Romano cheese
Salt and pepper, to taste
½ c. Bisquick or 6 Tbsp. flour and 1 tsp. baking powder

Peel and shred zucchini (or slice thin). Add onion, salt, pepper, parsley, cheese and Bisquick. Add eggs and mix well.

Using a large spoon, drop batter in oil, making small pancake-size patties. Fry until golden brown.

Mae Gagliano
Staten Island, New York • Commonwealth Edison

Index